# Two for
# the Road

Frederic Raphael

# Two for the Road

*Jonathan Cape*
*Thirty Bedford Square London*

00689006

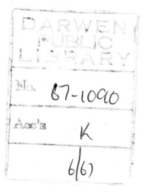

Printed in Great Britain
by Ebenezer Baylis and Son Limited,
The Trinity Press, Worcester, and London,
on paper made by John Dickinson and Co. Ltd.
Bound by A. W. Bain and Co. Ltd., London

*For Stanley*

# *Preface*

The choice between fiction and the cinema has long been regarded, for the writer, as a choice between God and Mammon. To write novels or stories (provided they are not tailored for the market) is acceptable both socially and morally, but to write for the movies is defensible only if one can parade starving children to mitigate the verdict of the aesthetic jury. I held this view myself, without much practical evidence, for a long time. Now, after a period of extensive involvement, I am bound to say that I have come to the conclusion that almost everything that has been said against script-writing is wholly justified. Will they chew you up and spit your boots out? If they get half a chance, yes. Is a producer a man who takes the only remaining bottle of water from a man dying of thirst in the desert and spits into it to improve the flavour? With a few exceptions, yes. Is a director someone who expects a round of applause when the sun rises in the morning? Yea, and when it goeth down at night. As a forcing ground for self-delusion, self-importance, greed, plagiarism, hypocrisy, vanity, hindsight, malice, treachery, impatience, superstition, sycophancy and fatty degeneration of the moral fibre, the cinema has few equals. In the light of this, of course, its attractions are obvious. Not only are writers able to practise these vices with rapidly maturing facility, but they are able to do so without the smallest twinges of conscience: crimes committed in outlaw territory are no crimes. There is nothing that so convinces a literary man that all scruples can be abandoned as the mention of a film company. He will rob them, give them short measure, offer them beads for gold and react with affronted surprise at any resentment the Barbarians show him for the treatment he has handed

7

them. Has he not done them a favour by visiting their benighted country at all?

At the best, those who still genuflect at the printed word treat the movies with that indulgent contempt which the British aristocracy used to show Americans: one associates with them because they have the money, but one pays them out by placing them a long way down the table. For every writer who has even the slightest of good words to say for films, there is a legion to bray its suspicious disgust. No novelist of whom I have ever heard has had anything favourable to say about the adaptation of his book for the screen. (In fact, of course, there is no obligation to sell one's work to film companies, though there is, among many pretentious writers, a strong compulsion to expiate one's greed by deriding the use made of it.) I am not claiming that the film companies are the innocent patrons and amiable sugar daddies of irresponsible and ungrateful writers. I am simply saying that a convenient double-standard of morality has been established and that it has come to excuse the failure of writers to take the cinema seriously. The style in which a business is run has become confused with the style in which films must be made. The inability or unwillingness to be imaginative in terms of film has become a virtue not so much because film is not an art as because it is an industry. The evidence may still point to the folly of associating with the bitch-Goddess of Hollywood or with any of the lesser whores who staff her provincial temples (for them the applause, for you the clap), but that is not at all the same thing as saying that the form itself is necessarily contaminated. The case against working in films is circumstantial.

It remains painfully strong. My first experience in films was as an underpaid, overworked and ignorant hack. I was filled only with a romantic desire to earn some money (I might as well have worked in a restaurant or a garage, for all that I cared about the end product), and then get away and write a novel. I had no critical or creative standards of my own; I knew what kind of writer I wanted to be, but I assumed you could only be the kind of script-writer other people wanted. I accepted, with a kind of masochistic relish, that one entered the business by working on the sort of film one would never dream of going to see. I was, I think it fair to say, more innocent than spineless. Earnest for artistic privacy, I could not believe that anything good could come out of creation by committee. In view of the committees into which one was recruited, it could be said that my doubts were priggish, but hardly that they were unwarranted. The Rank Empire was in its last grotesque stage as a major producing studio. In a period of slumping audiences and rising costs, the industry dozed in a dream of eternal boom. Convinced by every failure that it had the recipe for success, it launched more and more absurd follies and was already laying down their sister-ships before it had time to notice that they had, every one, sunk without trace. Aping the manners and ruthlessness, the mono-lithic vanities and blindnesses of the great American studios to which they had never been invited, the commanders of the crumbling bastions of British film-making set about blowing their already diminished resources with an appropriate mixture of Byzantine profligacy and Byzantine intrigue. It hardly adds to the credibility of those who still bleat for an independent British industry that they are nearly all of them the same men whose lack of enthusiasm, wit and passion scuppered the very craft from whose upturned wreckage they now proclaim their rights to new and more expensive commands. The independence for which these damp admirals still campaign has nothing to do with artistic independence whatever. It is a convenient argument, a happy prejudice to which to appeal, their suggestion that British art is being sacrificed at the altar of American greed, but there is precious little to make anyone who has worked in films believe that there is any truth in it. The artistic freedom which some independent British producers and directors have won has nearly always come from the confidence which American distri-butors have shown in their projects. In general, British sources of finance have always been reluctant to encourage originality. Those who want a British industry safe from American interest are, it may generally be assumed, those who want an artificial

9

lack of competition and who want to maintain a closed shop in which inefficiency, cliquishness and vulgarity can enjoy the subsidy or at least the protection of a falsely stimulated patriotism.

Remember the ridiculous mice which the mountainous monstrosity of Pinewood in its prime brought forth, and consider whether anything better could now be hoped for. Who will ever forget those days at Iver when, cloistered in the fumed oak dining-room (reminiscent of a golf club where no one ever paid his subscription), frightened producers blenched at the mere idea of any film which contained the smallest tincture of reality? 'Nothing genuine added' had to be the label on every confection. As at Byzantium, there was no choice between *proskynesis* and summary execution: the strongest went instantly to the wall; the servile lived to wilt again another day. Feasting their limp guests on rigid gammon and clotted potatoes, the cowed courtiers proposed unspeakable projects and dreamed less of fame or wealth (though both were pious hopes) than of a named slot in the car park. They ordered things differently, perhaps, at Ealing, though even there the flight from reality was fully booked. At least it served a creative route and did not merely circle the Emperor, dipping its wings. Films were made at Ealing, careers at Pinewood. Yet how complacently and self-admiringly parochial seem all but a handful of the famous Comedies! *Kind Hearts and Coronets* may be a masterpiece, but the determination of the majority of them to portray England peopled with characters and sustained by resolute dottiness played its part in encouraging, as it plainly derived from, the notion that the world owed Britain a living and that an inefficient Englishman was worth a dozen of your wily foreigners any day of the week. The Ealing style of acting has not had a good influence. It has endorsed the idea that a dozen crude impersonations are worth more than a single subtle reading. Guinness does not improve on keeping. It is without personal malice that I would claim that there is barely any film in which Sir Alec has appeared which does not bear the signs of deliberately uninquiring middlebrow calculation, not by any means necessarily stemming from him but instinct in the kind of thing in which he is likely to be asked to appear. If there is an academic tradition in British films (and I here include all those of David Lean, whatever their financial backing), Sir Alec is its main custodian and exponent. Without him, a number of bold and original ventures might never have come to life; with him, their boldness and their originality have been trimmed to conform to the very standards of good taste and good humour which they might have challenged. He is like some halfway Midas who turns everything he touches into semi-precious metal. His contemporary equivalent is Peter Sellers, who is a far more inventive talent, a creative mimic where Sir Alec was never more than an impressionist, but who has a similar baleful influence, though in a converse sense: if Sir Alec is to be in a film, the odds are that it will be good, even if he is bad; if Sellers is to be in it, that it will be bad, even if he is good. Neither of them inspire or, I suspect, have much stomach for serious work. Sir Alec mistakes technique for art and solemnity for seriousness; Sellers mistakes inconsistency for versatility and capriciousness for freedom. Both could be singular sources of creative opportunity and both have failed to become so. Dirk Bogarde, with less exceptional qualities, has lent himself to a far greater range of imaginative effort.

Nevertheless, the best achievements of both Sellers and Sir Alec render utterly puerile the pretensions of the British studios when I first went, tremblingly impressed, through their Sergeanted doors. There was no Independent Television then, none of the proliferation of independent producers – some driven by the bad breath of McCarthyism, others by financial and artistic opportunity, from their traditional haunts – which together today provide so much wider a market and so much less standardized a demand than screen-writers ever enjoyed before. Those who have been accustomed to subsidized easy pickings (and in this context those who have supped much sweetness from the miraculously unconsumed carcass of British Lion are scarcely the least pampered) may now complain of the domination of American capital, but who of us who had even the vaguest knowledge of those days would consent to go back to creating material for Tony

Wright and Jill Ireland and Maureen Swanson and Susan Beaumont and Anthony Steele? (True, there were talents like Richard Attenborough and Dirk Bogarde and Kenneth More, but the use to which they were put was often contemptible and rarely worth remembering. To think that only just over ten years ago *The Deep Blue Sea* was considered serious!) My own dim contribution to the prevailing ghastliness was to collaborate on a film which started as a light-hearted, if absurdly glamorized, story of the Cambridge of yellow waistcoats and beige playboys, of young Tories and old buffers, and which I helped to concoct with the zestful commercialism of one surprised to discover that earning a living could be even moderately enjoyable. How it turned into a square-wheeled vehicle for a German actor, who was more remarkable for his steadiness under a remorseless fire of old jokes than for any conceivable plausibility or humour in his delivery of them, provides a mere footnote to that long story of film subjects designed for one person, altered to fit another and finally proved to be a good fit only for someone with six arms and no head. (No method of resuscitation is so popular in executive circles as decapitation.) Not long afterwards, Rank abruptly jettisoned all its contract artists and proceeded to the policy of muddled patronage to which it is still haphazardly committed. Independent television sopped up most of the displaced talent and soon began to ape the employment methods and Caesaropapist tendencies of the shattered studios. Now it is BBC-TV and the four big independent companies who try to create by committee and formula and who tart up the triviality of what they really believe in by affectations of cultural devotion and public service. These groups have a cartel so powerful and so far beyond any public check that their authority over their employees, especially directors and writers, is unquestionable enough for them to experiment, like some Emperor, now indulgent, now ruthless, with all sorts of intimidatory techniques which either crush the rebellious by sudden fiat or smother the unusual with overdoses of maternalism. The tame house magazines, *Radio Times* for the literate, *TV Times* for those who need help with the long words, more and more pump out that unnatural gas which the fan magazines and the studio hand-out so willingly manufactured in the past and which slowly but surely deprives those who sniff it of the ability to know when their feet are on the ground and when they have become dangerously or irremediably beclouded. When ITV began, the hypocritical campaign which knew that only the promise of a quality service would secure its sponsors their licence to print money led drama departments to aim high. In large measure, it is only fair to say, the highbrows let them down, just as they often, more cynically, let the movies down. Because of the assumed primacy of the printed word, the 'serious' writers played with the new medium, tried to stick tired dramatic fragments or banal literary ideas into the new framework and dismissed it, rather than their own ineptitude, when they were a bad fit. (John Mortimer has pointed out, with somewhat disingenuous severity, how poorly most novels would stand the critical examination of public performance. It is not a fair standard because, of course, no novel is intended for such a test; what is intelligent, humorous or moving in private is often dull, twee or embarrassing when offered to a more numerous audience. Novels are not films or plays and cannot be measured by their standards, though I shall come to the ways in which these categorical divisions may not much longer be as 'natural' as it now seems.) I am not suggesting, incidentally, that highbrows are inevitably either dishonest or reactionary, merely that they are inclined to assume the immutability of literary categories and the inferiority, at all times, of any but purely verbal media. They despised the theatre until the cinema came along, radio until television. They often have good reasons for their hostility, but hardly less often they despise the cinema for its failure to admire what is neither cinematic nor admirable. The Age of Criticism has accustomed writers in particular to think in terms of a small informed public which will be more delighted by allusion than by self-justifying expression; it is hard to leave the protective stockade in which the esoteric have so long enclosed themselves. The habit of second-order comment, even in supposedly fictional work, is one of the great vices of contemporary writing. In film, the image must stand on its own (although, of course, the critical movement in the cinema, particularly strong just now, is trying to thicken the language of the movies for reasons which are, as I shall try to show, muddled and, though admirable, of transitory validity), and the writer cannot rely on a tradition of deference. If the motto of the established writer is 'What I have written, I have written,' the motto of the director, established or not, is 'What you have written, I have changed.' The kind of leverage which the writer can employ against the mutilation of his work by a book publisher is utterly futile against the film men. It is not, in any case, necessarily valid to assume that whichever form offers one greater authority is automatically the more considerable artistically, but in fact the leverage available to writers in the cinema is growing all the time and will, I should like to argue, eventually become very commanding indeed for those who have the courage and the wit to persevere.

People often ask whether the film-makers mess one's script about. The fact that they often do and that one does not have the legal right to prevent them does not mean that there is nothing one can do about it. (Though many 'sophisticated' writers find the pose of powerlessness extremely congenial: it excuses them from the moral (aesthetic) consequences of their labours.) Film people are at once ruthless and full of doubts; those who express clear and forceful opinions can often prevail over them. Their enthusiasm for the success of the moment, their penchant for buying at the top of the market, is but a sign of their insecurity. They long to procure a safe product. They like known quantities. (For much the same reason they would often sooner buy the rights of an expensive book than develop an original subject: to buy a bestseller gives them a 'property', something they can boast of having bought. They prefer to shop for their vegetables at Fortnum's than develop their own gardens; it's less trouble and it's more admirable and their friends assume they are both rich and discriminating.) The writer who works seriously in movies, who really wishes to protect his vision, has but to work on the psychological weaknesses of his colleagues, arguing his case reasonably where reason can convince, but working on the uncertainties and citing the past failures of his associates (all past films can be made to seem like failures) in order to strengthen his own case, should reason fail. I am not advocating a policy of sneers or calculated impertinence – it will simply land any newcomer in the street – but I am convinced that the writer of quality, who deserves to be heard, can find other ways of putting his case than calling his lawyer. I do not believe that the writer is always right and I would be very suspicious of anyone who worked with a director or producer in whose judgment he had no faith whatever. When he is in danger of being overborne where he is certain of his case, he has, if he has any personal force at all, an excellent chance of victory. The writer is, of course, most in danger (simply of being sacked) when he is hired to assemble but not to originate a screenplay. He is safest when the basic idea of the film and the vitality of its story and characters and symbolism rest in his imagination. To ditch the pilot in such circumstances is something which the vanity of the director and the myth that every writer can be replaced by another writer (what I have called the Theory of Unlimited Substitution) may cause them to do, but there is no shortage of cases when such lamentable consequences have followed that the writer has been recalled and vindicated. Film-writing has its political side and no politician can expect to stay in office without risk of interruption. One should fight remorselessly, but without rancour. Accept the seriousness of the medium, but not of its hierarchies. Naturally, that area of film-making in which this solemn advice applies is a small one, but then so is that area of publishing in which real imagination is welcome. My argument is not that anyone should work in films if he doesn't want to, only that no one should not work in films if he does want to, simply because he is intimidated by the power structure or because he is not the unquestioned master of the final product. No one would deny that only those with starving children or without taste or scruple could happily endure the systematic trivialization and the militant vulgarity of the old studio life. Even I, whose stomach was pretty strong in those days and who was able to anaesthetize myself by putting it all down to experience, finally became nauseated. It was an industry dominated by absurd rituals. Scripts were judged by the manner in which they were typed; numerology was important above all: producers flew into a rage if the numbering of the scenes was altered in a new version or if the wrong technical term was used, even if the idea involved was excellent.

Almost my last contact with the commercial cinema of the old days (and I do not mean that they are yet over) was when my agent asked me to go and see two American producers who had hit town and were looking for a writer to work on an epic. I had only one credit, as it is called, to my name: the unfunniest comedy of an unfunny era, the square-wheeled vehicle on which the German actor had been trundled to temporary oblivion. (In fact, an excellent straight actor, he has since made a number of worthwhile films.) I was planning to leave for Spain and a long spell of privacy, but I went. They handed me a thick thick script, beautifully duplicated, entitled *Damon and Pythias*. They were polite and they were friendly. They had a deal to make the picture, but the script needed work, they thought. What did I think? They had taken a room for me at the Grosvenor House in which I could decide what I thought and have coffee at the same time. I thanked them and told them that I would read it at home. They looked worried; they were in a hurry and the Grosvenor House was right by. So, I said, was home. Before I left, they briefed me with that authoritative anxiety which is typical of the Hollywood regular: 'Fred, we want you to realize that this is the story of two friends, that's the basic thing, the greatest friendship between two men that the world has ever seen, that's our story, that's what we want to tell, two guys who'll do anything for each other, don't let's lose sight of that.' I nodded and made for the door. 'Fred, one thing, one thing before you go, we've been thinking about our two characters, we've been doing some thinking and there's one thing you ought to bear in mind when you're reading the script: the way we see it now, where it says Damon that's Pythias and where it says Pythias, that's Damon. I wish you'd remember that.'

There is one infallible way of being hired as a rewrite man, should anyone ever wish a recipe for so crucifying a fate. It is to read the script and to blast it, with the sole reservation that there is basically a good idea somewhere in it. This method is especially successful if the producer is one of the authors, but it has never failed to my knowledge in any event. (There is an old story about a writer who was handed a colleague's script in the old days at Warner's/Paramount/20th Century or wherever and read it and came back and said 'I like it.' He never worked again.) Producers who 'have a deal' can make a living from a subject so long as it is somehow kept alive, so long as someone somewhere is working on it, so long as some writer thinks he can 'lick it'. The spiralling costs of mammoth films may seem the results of an industry gone mad, but the truth is that producers get richer through keeping a subject in the most expensive of oxygen tents than by allowing it to die economically. (In this respect, no great industry is that different; it is simply that the atomization of film produc- tion – the fact that each film is a separate enterprise from an accountancy point of view – makes its failures more spectacular and more ridiculous.) I abused the script of *Damon and Pythias* with the most constructive of hatchets and was, of course, offered the job of saving the enterprise: a ten-week guarantee at two, three and finally four hundred pounds a week. Having amused myself by manoeuvring the producers into accepting me, I re- sisted their generosity and left for Spain, shot for ever, as I thought, of the movies. (The film was later made, I heard, though I never discovered whether Damon was Pythias or Pythias Damon in the final version.) It was not a hard decision; I had not been very successful and I was ardent for privacy. I had decided that double-think was the inevitable language of the writer who tried to reconcile irreconcilables. I threw away my long spoons and would sup no more with the devil.

It is always less difficult to confess one's sins than to admit

17

one's naivetés. It was not until 1961, when we were in Paris for a few days, that I became acquainted with the work of Antonioni. I remember now looking in the *Semaine de Paris* for the week when we were there and picking out from among the potted synopses with which that magazine describes current films a cryptic sentence in which *L'Avventura* was said to be the story of a man who loses a girl and sets out to find her, only to fall in love with her best friend who is his companion in the search. We went and we went again. The impact of Antonioni's greatest film hit me with stunning and liberating force, so unexpected and so revolutionary was it, both in technique and content.

It seemed to me then and it seems to me now that *L'Avventura* finally disposed of the notion that there is a clear distinction in terms of absolute values between creative work in fiction and cinema. I thought when I was in my twenties that the movies would always be a world of bogus big deals and cynical short-term commercial calculations and, as I have said, there is no shortage of indications that it remains so. However, I believe that this situation may be on the point of altering and that very soon the writer who averts himself from film will be preserving a chastity of increasingly suspect value. One does not have to go the whole way with MacLuhan to see that the fluke of print has created a kind of closed shop for the imagination into which sooner or later light and all the media which involve light must be admitted. What many people fail to appreciate about the cinema is that the element of big deal is to a large extent also dependent on a kind of fluke. There is nothing to suggest that it is immutable. The machinery of the industry has in general been so expensive and so complicated to manipulate, has required such technical knowledge and such skilled staff to handle it and has cost so much, that a huge market has been necessary to finance its use. Mass entertainment will doubtless continue to be more and more expensive to create and doubtless it will continue to require an expanding audience. (The kind of production which *Two for the Road* has had certainly creates no hope of the early arrival of 'private cinema'.) On the other hand, although I am not interested – as I may not be justified – in claiming any originality in the manner of its conception, this script is perhaps unusual in having been written in private without many of those intrusions of commercial consideration which are normally associated with 'major' productions. The presence of stars need not be the sign that a film is bedevilled by commercial or temperamental demands. It may simply mean (though in this simplicity there are many complications) that it has the best possible performers in it. The script of *Two for the Road* was never influenced by hopes of securing either Albert Finney or Audrey Hepburn. It was seen, from the very beginning, as a film, not as a piece of tailoring.

A pretty journalist, with much experience of the movies, came to interview me recently for an article she was writing about 'The new image of Audrey Hepburn'. She, or at least her employers, imagined that deliberate plans had been made and *Two for the Road* subsequently set in motion in order to refashion Miss Hepburn (a definitive act of gilding the lily, if ever there was one). It is curious how even informed people can still believe that an industry as disorganized, as subject to sudden palace revolutions and as riddled by attacks of amnesia and faint-heartedness as the movies, is capable, nevertheless, of deliberately remodelling a star or of acts of intelligent and farsighted planning. Since the collapse of the studio armies, films have been dominated by marauding bands of *condottieri* of varying skill, force and cohesiveness. (The influence of the big agents is now hardly less important in collating and re-aligning talent than is that of the major distributors.) My interviewer's ideas were based, like too much thinking about movies, on concepts drawn from the days of the Pharaohs. The absurd flamboyance of the great age of ballyhoo has made a tone of supercilious sarcasm mandatory where uncritical deference – like that of *Sight and Sound* for Joseph Losey – cannot be sustained. Literary criticism and reviewing, on the other hand, is hampered by a tendency to excessive solemnity; although books now commonly contain 'fuck' and 'cunt', criticism never employs these words, never examines the

19

prevailing morality of its own terms, but has constant recourse to mandarin airs. I am not, of course, suggesting that 'fuck' is an essential critical term, merely that literary criticism is getting marooned among concepts which assume a stance that constricts any immediate contact with the work and which prevents a critique of modern culture being phrased in less than antique or academic terminology. Magazines like *King* offer an important opportunity here, though for possibly ramshackle motives, since they are prepared to come out with the unsayable and make a virtue of it. They encourage their critics to be themselves and if that is not always in specific cases what one would want them to be, one welcomes them for their indifference to the respectable. It is easy for them to become haunts of knocking copy, but it is not inevitable. A piece in *King* by Clancy Sigal at last came out with the unsayable about the National Theatre and blew a large breath of cold air through those complacent corridors before finally blowing its own brains out by a piece of blatant inaccuracy.

Nothing more clearly reveals the audience for which any writer is aiming than his style; a critic's unconscious limitations are best inferred from imagining the kind of people whose values he assumes and to whose common experience he seems to appeal. When the style becomes flip, the critic can be accused of pandering to the dismissive cynicism of his readers, but when it stays morbidly academic as most 'serious' criticism then one may justly guess that he is underwriting a conservative and monastic dilettantism. Those who write about films find it comfortable to assume the moral – equals aesthetic – turpitude of all but their Pantheon of Heroes. They may have some right on their side, but their certainty that all written material is the product of commercial calculation is actually an aspect of a bourgeois doctrine of which they are the unconscious victims and carriers. The film critics and their journalistic auxiliaries (if there is any distinction) are so determined to credit the directors with all the generative force that they act as a deterrent to the entry of serious writing into the cinema. We need an aesthetic – i.e. a creative morality – which accepts and encourages the notion of collaborative art, despite its dangers and the difficulty of establishing its standards, and which does not rely supinely on the convenient myth of the divine right of directors. Film critics have accepted an aesthetic of authorship from literary and that of 'performance' from theatrical criticism. They have yet to find a standard (and hence a place) for visual writing, to coin an unhappy phrase. They have yet to see how the solitary theoretical imagination can be of vital significance in the cinema. It should be possible to encourage writers to break out of the congealed customs of the industry and to create blueprints for films with the same facility and lack of practical consideration with which novelists propose ideas to themselves. The habit of waiting for commissions aborts imaginative work in the cinema. The lack of 'impossible' projects has limited the frontiers of the form. (One thinks of the stimulating effect of the bizarre fancies of, for instance, Gordon Craig and Antonin Artaud in the theatre.) A certain lack of finish, a certain excess of invention – a kind of rhetoric, exhortation rather than achievement – would always be likely to accompany these projects: they would be envelopes, capable of taking in more material than they already enclosed, rather than tables of contents. They would have a certain openness. All scripts must. (*Two for the Road* was shot almost as written, but the locations and the imaginative attempts of the actors when they came actually to play the scenes and the eye of the director properly and inevitably affected the actual filming. In this case I thought I saw a complete vision of the film at the time I wrote it, but I would be foolish to imagine that when it came to actual shooting the material created would conform without deviation to the ideas which I had projected in the cinema of my mind.)

I do not think that the writer can much longer claim that he has no place in film-making simply because he is liable to be ground up by the mincer into which his talent is fed. When Hollywood began to crack up, the stars and the directors were the first people to realize that they had nothing to lose but their long-term contracts and that no law of nature obliged them to sit like taxis on the rank waiting for a whistle from studio heads. Writers, however, have continued to embrace their bonds and to accept the shibboleth that they can strike no other attitude but that of wry and gold-hungry subservience. Admittedly, it is still true that it is almost impossible for a writer to sell his work for films without allowing control of it to pass out of his hands. No director (and no production company) is prepared to be contractually obliged to put all or even any part of the written dialogue or action on to the screen without the right to cut. This is hardly surprising to anyone who knows anything about the business. The technique of film is closely involved with the technique of editing. What is in doubt here, it seems to me, is not whether the writer should therefore renounce films but whether he should not advance a great deal more boldly into them.

It is largely because the director has been the only person whom the industry has been unable *entirely* to control (he is the guardian who cannot be guarded) that he has seemed to provide the only creative spark in an otherwise quasi-automatic industrial production line. The writer has nearly always been an employee whose work has been subject to constant change, revision and often emasculation, usually by the director and producer (who will later say they made the film) before a single foot has been shot.

The time cannot long be delayed when technical changes will alter the whole balance of the movies. Already machines exist in America which are able to tape-record both sound and vision in 'natural' conditions. As soon as these machines become commonplace (and I doubt whether it will take very long), it will be possible to create films without the ponderous paraphernalia of studio equipment and staff which have so far made the imagination of film-makers subject, except in exceptional circumstances, to the exigencies of the budget-makers and the supposed demands of the mass audience. Books need not remain the sole respectable expression of the writer's imagination, nor can the higher standards continue to be applicable only to those who commit their ideas to the printed word. How long can the bookshelf, the easel painting and the record cabinet remain the sole repositories of art in the home?

(Networked television may be enjoying a far more fleeting prosperity than most people suppose. Television cannot rise to individual taste but can only satisfy, like some huge snack bar, the famished appetites of those too footsore to go any further. Always a journalistic medium and always, in creative terms, a verbal one, it is more likely to become the newspaper-magazine of the future than its characteristic art form. In passing, the medium is *not* the message.) I hope for a time when writers will become each one of them *auteurs* in a less vague sense than those directors on whom *Sight and Sound* and *Cahiers du Cinéma* so recklessly lavish their political honours. The tedious perversity of the one and the tinselly sycophancy of the other are tickled to find in a capricious variety of directors those vague signs of individuality which, quite rightly, though they misapply this insight, they believe to be the signs of significant activity in any creative field. Their genius for shortsightedness and their eager desire to cringe at the feet of any god lead them to think that the director alone can be the vessel of that vital spark which breathes life into mortal clay. The cult of the director springs directly out of the desire to apply a finished aesthetic theory to an art form which has barely emerged from its curiously haphazard genesis. (God knows it was a rough beast, its time come round at last, that shambled towards Hollywood to be born.)

An intensely bourgeois theory lies at the bottom of the unimaginative sycophancy of many highbrow critics of the cinema. In spite of John Berger, they have fallen entirely for the image of the critic as a sole voice crying in the wilderness, 'Prepare ye the way of the *auteur*.' Forgetful of, for instance, the craftsmen of Chartres and Autun, they assume that a work of art must be the consequence of the activity of a single mind. The literary tradition of criticism, from which they affect to have escaped, imprisons them. They make cinema criticism respectable by running their trains of thought up and down the doctrinal rails

23

laid down by the myth of directorial sovereignty: the 'subject' is matter, whatever lies inert beneath the director's finger before he begins creating, and the director is Mind which moves and gives it its blessing. In fact, except in cases where the writer and the director are the same person, the director is almost always the servant either of the industry or of an idea of himself far more than he is the sole and urgent author of a private vision. The 'creative freedom' cantingly ascribed to directors is nearly always won by the producer (and sometimes even by the writer). The independent producer is, in the Anglo-Saxon cinema, no less a vessel of magic, at least commercially speaking, than the director. Those who suppose that successful directors choose their next subject and have their choices automatically endorsed by a grateful industry show little knowledge of the practicalities of production. Directors, of course, eagerly endorse the myth of their own autocracy. Casting which has been wished upon them is passed off as the consequence of their brilliant insistence; every fortuitous circumstance is said to be the result, if it earns praise, of their singular foresight; no good idea originated with anyone else and any defect in the final product is blamed either on the producer or on the writer. The insular toadies who promote certain directors, often on the thinnest of justifications, to the status of Masters pander to a vanity which would be laughable if it were not so destructive. *Modesty Blaise*, for instance, a pot-boiler which never managed to come to the simmer, was treated with grave appreciation by critics who applauded every dismal miscue as if it were the most subtle of innovations. So starved are the cinema critics of anything susceptible of serious analysis that they are obliged to fantasize a few jumped-up *auteurs* into Masters and then to deduce that whatever a Master does is a masterpiece. They still cling with a touching monotheism to the idea that all the visual content of a film is thought up by the director after the writer has supplied the words. Because dialogue was, in the heyday of Hollywood, sometimes written independently of the shooting script, the simple-minded pietists assumed that things remain so and that the directors are for ever saving the script from the incurable literariness of the writers. In fact, the writer is far more often battling against the timidity of the director (and the producer) than he is stimulated by their urge to 'make it new'. If directors were half as clever in suggesting ideas as they are in culling credit for other people's, they would be inventive indeed. Writing, in the broadest sense of theorizing, and not directing (in the sense of coming in to organize the shooting of someone else's work), will prove to be the key in the future of film as an art form.

The arrival of words in the cinema was in many ways a retrograde advance. Those who had been able to devise pictorial stories were cowed by the literary associations of the verbal, and a long series of tedious and loquacious films, with undue deference shown to dialogue (whose author often turned out to be an inept dramatist or an imported gold-digging highbrow), led pictures to lose their force. The grafting of literary imagination was never willingly undertaken and never successfully 'took'. The middlebrow era arrived and with it the dilution or damaging of two vital influences: that of the untutored vernacular, the 'immigrant's view' of the world (particularly, of course, of America) with all its curious overstated fears and hopes, violence and passion; and, on the other hand, that of intelligence and imagination working at the higher levels of sublimation. It is no accident that the *Cahiers* critics use the word *auteur*, for they are, in an understandable confusion of terminology, looking for the signs of non-literary intelligence or authority at work in film. Where their theory is inadequate, I think, is that it is essentially a sentimental one (it looks back) and, reacting against the excessive veneration for literature in France, it is inclined to be altogether too frightened of the signs of conscious intelligence. The *Cahiers* critics' sentimentality leads them to think that there was some kind of noble savage who roamed happily before the days of chat, who never suffered from the sin of having read a book and to whose non-verbal vision every film must either approximate or fail. (The tendency to underrate the informed intelligence may be seen most clearly in François Truffaut's *Fahrenheit 451*, where he attempts to show the banausic horrors of a society entirely hostile to the written word. He succeeds, presumably against his conscious intentions, in making the reading of books and the literary intelligence seem so tedious and priggish that one loses all sympathy with the story's worthy outlaws, in whose obstinate memories books still live. Truffaut's self-admiring and self-deprecating humour leads him to include a copy of *Cahiers du Cinéma* in the pile of banned books consigned to the flames. In doing this, he admits the literary origins of *Cahiers'* anti-literary bias and reveals its position to be a transitory rather than a definitive one.)

What Truffaut as critic and creator has often successfully attempted to do is to rescue the cinema from those literary intelligences which would affect to do it a favour. If the cinema is to be an art form (in other words if it is to express the total vision of those who work in it), then it patently cannot tolerate being patronized: it cannot suffer gladly the position of gaudy mistress with a man who is truly wedded to another style of life. However, if I am right, the division which sees a writer as properly engaged in novels, short stories, criticism, poetry and even plays, but which regards him as taking part in an utterly different activity if he involves himself with film, must eventually lose its force. (It is curious to notice how propriety always endorses those forms of life which are just beginning to fall into obsolescence.) Henry James imagined himself to be stepping into some moral mine-field when he committed himself for a brief and inglorious season to the theatre, and he did so in part perhaps for public glory (in other words, out of envy) and partly because he imagined that it would make him rich enough to be able to devote himself to fiction for ever after. Nowadays the theatre, possibly because of the tedium which is its constant concomitant, enjoys the approval of the genteel aesthetic. It is the nostalgia for religion which leads this kind of lay service to enjoy the reluctant subsidy of the state and the unthinking devotion of the middlebrow. (It is a rare play which manages to be less tedious than the interminable intervals which divide it.) There is also the relentless self-promoting skill

26

of the actors. If plays were as boring to perform as they are to witness, the theatre would vanish overnight. It is only on the rarest occasions that I would not happily be translated from attending a good play to seeing a bad film.

The main reason that the theatre remains attractive to the writer is that his words, since it is a wordy platform, are granted some kind of scriptural authority. If film production were to cease to be as complicated as it now is, the whole ponderous grindstone of the manufacturing mill would cease in large measure to crush the creative talent. Not only would writers not necessarily serve an industry bound to sell millions of seats in order to recover its costs, but at the same stroke they would cease to be involved in the necessity of explaining and justifying everything which did not serve profitable ends. It would then no longer be necessary for the *Cahiers* critics and their twee imitators to look in the dark recesses of the commonplace for faint traces of personality on which to bestow the accolade of auteurship. The bird-brain would no longer be the largest in the game.

It is the tradition of the theatre, in my view, rather than the tradition of the novel, which is the main enemy in the creation of films. It is the architectural tradition of the theatre which insists that people sit in rows, massed together, and which makes the programmes subject to the commercial consideration of getting as many audiences as possible into and out of the cinema in a day. It is the theatre which makes actors still declaim their lines and which insists on the public propriety and public intentions of what is shown and said. It is the theatre which makes actors still count the number of lines in a part and seem quite indifferent to the silent opportunities for a kind of acting often more revealing, more intense and more true than any theatre can sponsor.

It is still almost unquestioningly assumed, at least outside the mammoth productions of, for instance, the state-sponsored Russian cinema, that films should run for no longer than the bottoms of the audience can tolerably endure at a single sitting. It is assumed that one must cut a long story short (see Robert Bolt's introduction to his screenplay of *Dr Zhivago*) and it is assumed that a scene must have a *theatrically* dramatic form. But what if films ran for eight, ten or even twenty-four hours? It may happen not because of the springing of ever more plush seats, but because the audience will be sitting at home and will watch as much of the film as they feel able to enjoy or take in at a single sitting and will then switch it off and resume on another occasion. What could be less surprising? No one sits down and reads even the most time-serving of 80,000-word novels at a single sitting. One of the greatest obstacles to imaginative complexity in the cinema is the fact that audiences can never go back and check an earlier passage as a reader can when involved in a novel. (The films of Alain Resnais are perhaps best understood as attempts, by reiteration and anachronistic juxtaposition, to make the audience aware of earlier events and possibilities which a responsible and responsive reader would derive either by going back in the text or by paying close attention to the inner stitching of the language in a particular passage.) I am not suggesting necessarily that films will become more like Resnais's – in fact if the viewer is able to turn back himself, a greater simplicity of line may accompany the greater sophistication of content for which I am looking. In simple terms, films will be run like tapes, and like tapes will be reversible. In the same way the film-maker, like the novelist, will not be afraid of losing his audience through the publication of passages which may be tedious but which contain elements of the narrative which seem to him to be of importance. He will be able to comfort himself, if it is a comfort, by the knowledge that the bored viewer, like the bored reader, will be able to skip.

Once the theatrical stranglehold is broken, it will be possible for films to find new rhythms. A film called *Darling*, of which I wrote the script, suffered badly from the pace imposed on it by the race to make it entertaining. I would have preferred the film to have been a great deal longer and a great deal duller. The compression of a life full of fears, doubts and panic made it appear a giddy roundabout of contemporary delights. The girl's superficiality was superficially analysed, where an analysis in depth of her and her environment could have offered a wholly different and more significant perspective for it. The same incidents might have occurred, but they would have been spaced in such a way that they would not have created the same impression of resolute reaching for effect. The erotic would have been liberated from the spectacular and where allusion became sensationalism, the private version of *Darling* might have been much more explicit, more openly true and so avoided that rhetoric of sexuality which led to overstatement. The still photographer, the novelist and even the pornographer (in an idealized sense!) have more to offer in the liberation of the cinema from the theatrical stereotypes wished on it by public performance than excessive veneration for imprisoned Masters. (The 'underground' cinema, shrilly proclaiming the novelty of tedium, is an important critical stage in the assault on theatrical cinema and on the categorical distinctions between art forms. It is in a certain sense asking philosophical-aesthetic questions about the distinctions between picture, image, story, canvas and poster art, sound and noise and so on. No one, I imagine, would wish to be faced with this style of questioning much longer, but the questions are not necessarily without value.)

The eight-hour film will draw its extra intensity from a more concentrated use of language and visual image, rather than from a more spectacular story or staging. It will not, one hopes, be more realistic (in the sense of documented, unshaped naturalism), but it will, it seems likely, be charged with a kind of accuracy which is rare in cinema now. It will, for reasons of practical economy, be more like chamber music. Actors, when they are professionals, will be asked for a higher standard of musicianship than they now generally offer. The habit of dubbing and post-synching has led to a continued indifference on the part of actors (and directors) to the absolute pitch essential to the correct *imaginative* interpretation of speech. Directors still fail to realize that a speech hopelessly mis-sung can never be properly post-synched; the shape of speech affects the shape of the face, the cast of the body, the movement of the flesh, and mere adjustment of the sound can never rectify the visual-auditory complex which is the cinematic image of a man or woman saying something. The obsession with story, with telling, gets in the way constantly of the film-maker's proper art, which is showing. (The distinction is, in a certain sense, academic, but it is time that the pretensions of those who complacently mangle what they will call 'mere dialogue', without any understanding that speech is also action, were plainly challenged.) The new private cinema will, hopefully, not be in the hands of 'interpreters'. The simplicity of the new machinery will deliver us from the proliferation of technical assistants in whose management, far more than in his intellectual or artistic powers, lies the present dominance of the director. A Napoleon complex will no longer be the occupational neurosis of those who conduct films. Intensity will gain from the need no longer to explain to a shoal of jealous sceptics exactly what one's meaning is. (The novelist is not obliged to 'justify'.) Given the faith of a relatively small number of people, the author will be able to proceed with total command, provided he is capable of the creative act at all. I cannot say what the cost of the new films might be (this is a very hypothetical situation, confident though I am that it will come about), but there is no reason why copies should not be sold much as novels are now, though they are bound, in the beginning, to be expensive. Suppose, however, that copies could be made quite cheaply (obviously 'libraries' would soon grow up), there is no reason why a film should not be 'published', *mutatis mutandis*, and why large advances should not be made to the author to complete them. The book publishers are now very similar to 'producers' in the film business; they are able to launch more 'shows' because each production costs very little. It is not that they are more daring, simply that they can back a great many horses, while the minimum stake of the film producer is so large that he must decide on a very few. (The restrictive practices which beggar the film business will, of course, be exploded by the new techniques. The size of a film unit is grotesquely disproportionate to the numbers really required. Demarcation amounts virtually to a protection racket.)

The freedom of the novel writer has been more due to the cheapness of printing and the comparatively small risk involved in making a commercial mistake than to any essential moral or aesthetic quality which the writing down of words or the verbal telling of stories could be held to have. Novelists have for too long excused their slovenliness, their ineptitude and their lack of originality by claiming some special status for literary art. I was recently infuriated by a publishing lady who saw nothing disreputable in telling me that she thought that most novelists wrote their books in the hope of selling the film rights. I denied indignantly any such motive on my own part (sanctimonious in the comfortable knowledge that no film company has even shown the faintest flicker of interest in any book of mine), but I suppose that there must have been some justice in what she was saying. If so, the primacy of the novel as the sacred vehicle of personal expression is even more in hazard than I imagined (evidently many writers have long since sold the pass), and any aesthetic defence of literature as inevitably of a higher order than the film must become suspect, even if at this moment I personally am still inclined to accept it.

From my own personal point of view, *Two for the Road* represents an important stage in the breakdown of certain psychological inhibitions. Although the origins of a work are of much less consequence than most polite or curious inquirers lead artists to think, there was to me something significant in the fact that the idea for the film came to me much more like the idea for a story than like the idea for some kind of public show. While it would be silly to pretend that writers are not interested in seeing their books sold (even the most dedicatedly self-destructive and world-rejecting authors may be seen asking in bookshops for copies of their own books), it is true that most serious authors regard the composition of novels as entirely uninfluenced by sales considerations. On the whole, film-writers have never pretended to be indifferent to the market. *Two for the Road* would, I think, have been written as a film regardless of whether anyone showed any interest in performing it. In this, through impulse rather than virtue, I found myself behaving very differently from the kind of screen-writer whom Mrs Hitchcock calls the true professional, the one who never types a word without seeing money on the table.

We were driving down the N6 towards Lyon and the sun for the *n*th time in our lives when I remarked how odd it would be to overtake ourselves as we were in the days when we were penniless hitch-hikers on the same road. No sooner had the thought come to me than the opportunities it offered for a cinematic development – going one way in space and in all directions in time – became very obvious.

One of the things which films have so far been least able to do is to avoid the tendency to 'pastoralize' emotional relationships. The *coup de foudre* is the stock form of vital sexual encounter. The present is everything, and both the past and future are sacrificed to it. The 'happy' ending is a pastoral conclusion; it less assumes a satisfactory future, though conventional morality has led it to seem to do so, than signifies the end of the game by showing it at its most 'perfect' moment. Stories about marriage have suffered from the excessive schematization which has divided film stories into 'comedy' and 'serious' and film-makers into 'commercial' and 'art'. You cannot be serious, in general, unless you show a marriage at disaster stations; you must be joking if you show one that is capable of survival. (The only film which I recall that showed a marriage that was at once desirable and, for the moment, impossible was *Edouard et Caroline*, which I have not seen for a long time, but which had a kind of larky seriousness that suggested very well the possible rewards of not only lusting after people but knowing them well.)

I hoped in *Two for the Road* to return to simplicity. *Darling* had stretched to include too much, had tried to be too comprehensive and to make too large a statement. I looked not directly at our life but at the kind of life we had led and at the kind of incidents which had occurred in it. I had no big idea. The habit of over-statement, the zeal for types and for a sort of tarty sophistication, seemed to me to have displaced human drama and the humour of character (rather than situation) from the screen. I wanted to tell the story of two people who had no awareness that they had been commissioned to be funny or serious, no mission to show the impossibility of human communication or the desirability of the married state, who had no intention of taking part in a comedy or of being involved in a tragedy if they could help it and who, within the limited freedom a writer can afford his characters, simply lived their lives. Film-writing is bedevilled by the urge of directors and producers to calculate exactly what category a film shall fall into and to call for a script which will leave critics and audience in no doubt. (The publicity people were very disturbed when I couldn't tell them what kind of a film *Two for the Road* was; the trade magazines must have a one-word, check-list designation. I said it was a film, but that wouldn't do at all.) The best people know exactly what shaped pill they are trying to feed the audience. Even Karel Reisz, having elected to make *Morgan* a comedy, could not suffer a laughless second to pass; instead of allowing the story to have real feeling, instead of showing what was truly funny and what was truly sad (hardly tragic), he stamped on our ribs trying to tickle us to death. On the other hand, not a glimmer of humour (contact with contingency) was allowed to mottle the glum surface of *This Sporting Life*, in which tragedy was earnestly and implacably stalked until it dropped. Both subjects, worthily undertaken by worthy men, suffer as much from *a priori* decisions as the most banal situation comedy. Their essential quality is lifelessness.

I do not for a second mean to suggest that *Two for the Road* conveys as important a message as either of these two masterpieces (nor do I for a second mean to deny it), but it is at least an attempt to ignore the categorizations which balkanize screen-writing and to aim directly at the creation of a film without gift-wrapping it for the art or the vulgar market. Joanna and Mark don't stand for anything, don't illustrate anything, don't *mean* anything. It does not follow that there is no moral to be drawn from their fond conflict (it seems to me that, in the end, *Two for the Road* is some sort of wry testimonial for marriage or at least for involvement as against having it off), but I resisted the temptation to intellectualize the situation, to make the film more serious by making it more flip, or more artistic by making it more solemn. There is, of course, a high degree of stylization. It was inevitable if so long a time-span was to be covered; unity had to be imposed by selection of incidents and by giving the dialogue a kind of shorthand (this often happens, of course, in the language of a long relationship and the loss of this language is not the least painful consequence of a break-up: remember 'Sollocks' in *Private Lives*). If things had been different, the story of Mark and Joanna could have been treated at inconceivably greater length and they might then have turned into less 'holiday' people. Quite literally, one could have covered their home life, one could have taken some of the gloss off them. The development of a long and serious relationship (in which the two people seek understanding as well as comfort or passion) is an obvious subject for the eight-hour film, just as it has long been the basic subject of the novel. *Two for the Road* can be nothing more than a trailer for such a work, theoretically speaking, looking at it, in other words, merely as a script. The finished film is, in this regard, an entirely different matter. For me personally, the script remains an important stage towards an imaginative synthesis.

The distinction between writing for the cinema and merely being a writer becomes hardly worth making once the inhibitions which prevent a writer from proposing a film to himself in the same way as he might embark on a novel are swept away. As soon as the technicalities of shooting are simplified, many more writers (though of course never all) will take to the blank screen with no less facility than they now apply themselves to the blank page. The director who interprets work but does not originate it will, I hope, become as unimportant in this perhaps always specialized area as the ghost writer. It is still a joke in literary circles to mention the man who always wanted to write but could never think of a plot; it may not be long before the director who is incapable of imagining a character or of developing a situation will become as foolish a figure. The director is in many cases no

34

less a theatrical hangover than the rows of seats and the 'get-out' figure. If he is a creator, he is in the Anglo-Saxon cinema often not much more than the pastrycook whose baroque curlicues hide the pedestrian recipe of the shop cake his sugar conceals. In fact, once the gold dust of banal enthusiasm has been blown aside, it can be seen that, even as things are, the only directors whose work positively excites the imagination tend to be, if they are not exclusively, those who do not rely on their writers and who, since this is the only way to avoid such reliance, are in large part writers themselves.

There will no doubt always be public cinema and there will always be a place, no doubt, for the director who can achieve spectacular effects and to whom applause no less than money will be the supreme objective. There will always be a public for those to whom publicity matters, though perhaps those who lack real imagination themselves and whose urge is always for effect are in more danger than they imagine. Coming up on their flank are flamboyant techniques, like that of all-round (360°) cinema, and even the three-dimensional image which will ask of them a great deal more than the kind of transferred theatricality on which their reputations are so often based. The new generation of authors in the cinema must be wary of becoming literary in a bad sense. Although 'adaptation' will doubtless have a place (and no one wants to make prescriptive rules), free composition directly for the screen should become the normal style. In the commercial cinema, the 'original' is a rarity, for reasons that I have already suggested. In future, the film-maker will not want to go through the laborious and often only half-baked reheating of literary matter. He will compose on the screen of his mind directly in visual and *heard* terms.

*   *   *

I have refrained from decorating the script with mystifying camera directions, which might have given it a more impressive air, or with more descriptive matter, which might have made it more luscious. It is printed as it was written, with the addition only of one or two locations which I never specified but which add much to the final film. The faults of the screenplay are entirely mine; it goes without saying that many of the virtues of the film itself are those of Stanley Donen, the most tactful of producers and the most intuitive of directors, and that you will, I fear, look in vain on the printed page for the magic and vitality which Audrey Hepburn and Albert Finney brought to the playing of Joanna and Mark.

# Two for the Road

1. EXT. *ROMNEY MARSH. DAY.*

*A small village on the marsh on a sunny morning. A bevy of old, black limousines with a wedding party in it is just pulling away from the gate.*

*A white Mercedes zooms into the village and comes down through a couple of angry gear-changes to confront the departing limousines. It bumps on to the pavement and jinks past the party until it comes face to face with the newly-weds.*

*The couple in the Mercedes,* MARK *and* JOANNA WALLACE, *are very good to look at and radiate the confidence of success, at least at first sight.* MARK *has a knitted cap on his head.* JOANNA *wears a silk scarf floating about her ears. Her eyes look out hugely and humorously.*

*The two in the Mercedes sit, for a moment, face to face with the two rather puddingy young people in the hired limousine.*

JOANNA (*whispers sideways*): They don't look very happy.
MARK: Why should they? They just got married.

> *The limousine* CHAUFFEUR *is forced to back up by* MARK'S *cold intransigence. The Mercedes, with another fancy gear change, hurtles through the gap and is gone up towards a hump-backed bridge.*

2. EXT. *LYDD AIRPORT. DAY.*

*The Mercedes, in close shot, suddenly seems to go up a steep hill (as if it had just hit the hump-backed bridge) and then there is a bump and as we ease back we see that in fact the car is being driven up a ramp into the nose of a Channel air ferry by one of the uniformed* DRIVERS. *We pan round to include the airport terminal and zoom in on the* V.I.P. *lounge.*

3. INT. *V.I.P. LOUNGE, AIRPORT. DAY.*
*Drinks are being placed in front of* MARK *and* JOANNA.

OFFICIAL: We hope you enjoy your trip, Mr Wallace – and your wife.

MARK: Thanks a lot.

> *The* OFFICIAL *goes out.*

MARK: Well, well! I suppose we have Maurice to thank for this. What're you doing?

> *She is passing her gloved hand over the top of the drinks.*

JOANNA: Just trying to discover where the strings are attached. (*She lifts her glass.*) We hope you enjoy your trip, Mr Wallace –

MARK (*doubtfully*): And my wife?

> JOANNA *looks at him and then sips, smiling to herself.*

MARK: You're entirely too suspicious about Maurice. What harm'd he ever do us?

JOANNA: He hounds us.

MARK: Hounds us?

JOANNA: He hounds us.

MARK: Nonsense.

> *The* OFFICIAL *now enters bearing a telephone on a long lead.*

OFFICIAL: Monsieur Maurice Dalbret for you, Mr Wallace, from St Tropez.

> JOANNA *goes and whispers to the* OFFICIAL, *while* MARK *starts talking.*

MARK (*to* JOANNA): He hounds us. (*Into phone*) Maurice, I told you. Of course we could have flown direct, but we wanted a few days on our own – Joanna and me. My wife. Yes. It's too late to change – anyway I want the car down there –

> *Meanwhile,* JOANNA, *by the window, is on another phone which has been brought in by the* OFFICIAL.

JOANNA (*smiling warmly, into the phone but in a slightly grand manner*): Yes, darling, of course we will. Of course we won't! Something lovely. Promise! And you'll take care of Granny, won't you? Yes, and Nanny. Take care of everyone. Daddy's just …

MARK: Three days – three – nothing's going to fall down. We have to fly. (*Shouts*) Fly … but that makes nonsense of the whole spatial concept – (*shouts*) Spatial concept! (*giving up*) It messes up the whole lousy design. I'll see you in three days.

> *He looks up to see* JOANNA *is holding out the phone to him.*

MARK (*irritably*): Yes? Now who is it?

JOANNA: Caroline.

MARK (*puzzled*): Caroline?

JOANNA: Caroline Wallace. (*Pause*) Your daughter.

MARK: Oh Caroline! (*takes the phone*) Caroline, how's my girl?

> *The roar of engines drowns the rest.*

## 3a. EXT. *RUNWAY. DAY.*
*The car ferry plane takes off.*

## 4. INT. *THE PLANE. DAY.*
MARK *sitting with his briefcase on his knee, a few architect's drawings (rough) spread on it. He makes a note or two with a pencil.*

JOANNA *leans back against her seat and closes her eyes. The* STEWARDESS *comes along with cigarettes.*

STEWARDESS: Cigarettes?

> MARK *shakes his head, concentrating on his papers. The* STEWARDESS *goes.* JOANNA *opens her eyes wide and studies* MARK.

JOANNA (*quietly*): Did you pick up your passport?

> *He nods and goes on reading, patting his pocket for his passport as he does so. He frowns, pats more frantically. He becomes increasingly desperate.*

MARK (*attempts to leap up, but is held back by his belt, which he hurriedly unfastens*): I'm sorry. We shall have to turn back. I've left my passport. We shall have to go back –

STEWARDESS: I'm sorry – are you sure?

MARK: I've got a most important conference I have to go to and I can't –

*MARK stumbles into silence as he sees JOANNA holding up the missing passport.*

JOANNA (*reads from it*): Mark Wallace, born 1933 – occupation architect?

*He makes a pressed-lips, mock-furious face at her. He sighs and takes the passport.*

JOANNA: Now how about buying me some cigarettes?

*We sense between them a kind of throttled intimacy: their jokes spring from their understanding of each other, but a kind of cloud prevents real warmth from getting through. MARK signals for the cigarettes, as the STEWARDESS comes back.*

MARK: I'm sorry. It's just that Maurice –

JOANNA: Has managed to persuade you that it's absolutely essential that we get to St Tropez by the day before yesterday. Why you always have to be taken in –

MARK (*imitating Bogart*): That's my nature, sweetheart.

*JOANNA lights a cigarette and rolls the cellophane of the packet between her fingers.*

MARK: Look, do you want me not to work? Is that what you want?

*JOANNA shrugs faintly.*

MARK: We're not going on like this for the rest of our lives.

*JOANNA looks away. MARK tries to work.*

MARK (*flies at her*): I just wish you'd stop sniping.

JOANNA: I haven't said a word.

MARK: Just because you use a silencer doesn't mean you're not a sniper.

*JOANNA fires at him suddenly with her fingers. He is not amused. She sighs and looks out of the window. MARK affects to go on working. JOANNA turns her wedding ring round and round on her finger. She looks down.*

5. EXT. *CHANNEL AND CROSS-CHANNEL STEAMER. DAY.*
*Top shot,* JOANNA'S P.O.V. *The steamer cleaves through the clear, blue water.*

JOANNA (*over*): You haven't been happy since the day we met, I know. If only you were ten years younger and you knew what you know now!
MARK: You can say that again.

6. INT. *THE PLANE. DAY.*
JOANNA *stares full at* MARK, *her eyes cold with tears of anger. His image is blurred. She looks out of the window again.*

7. EXT. *CHANNEL STEAMER. DAY.*
*A grey day.* MARK *is leaning against the deck rail, watching the horizon slip up and down. Start on his new and heavy walking boots. He is wearing hit-the-road clothes — levis, tartan jacket-shirt, loose-knit sweater. There is a small baggage bundle over his shoulder and a camera swings from his fist. It is twelve years earlier.*

*The usual gangs of* TOURISTS *are ambling about (we notice one* ENGLISHMAN *striding it, military fashion, round the deck),* TEACHERS *in batches,* CAMPERS *hung with pots and pans,* MAP READERS, *the whole crowd. As* MARK *watches, the parade is joined by a group of eight English* GIRLS *several of them quite attractive, some not. They file through into the saloon. Next to last is* JOANNA. *She looks at* MARK *and he at her without the faintest sign of recognition and without any great evidence of magic communion.*

8. INT. *BAR. THE STEAMER. DAY.*
*The* GIRLS *are lined up on the bar stools having drinks, snacks, etc. We start on* PAT WAINWRIGHT, *a pretty, plump girl, who is itching. She wriggles and scratches.*

PAT: I think it must be an allergy.
JACKIE: Scratching won't help.

> JACKIE *is the dark, glamorous one, the leader of the group.*

SALLY: Maybe it's something you've eaten.

PAT: I haven't eaten anything.

JOANNA (*turning a page of the magazine she's reading, not looking up*): Maybe it's something you haven't eaten. Maybe it's something you need.

PAT: It's possible, I suppose.

> PAT *looks up and meets* MARK's *unblinking stare. She blushes. She looks at* JACKIE. MARK *is sitting on the far side of the bar. There is a showcase of sandwiches between him and the* GIRLS.

MARK (*to the* BARMAN): And I'll have one of those.

> *He is sipping a beer, but gestures to the sandwich case. The* BARMAN *taps with the plastic tongs – this or this or this?*

MARK: Any one'll do. I'm not particular.

> *The* GIRLS *are on to the double meaning and giggle slightly to each other.* JOANNA *continues to read* Music & Musicians. *The hooter goes.*

## 9. INT. *THE STEAMER. DAY.*

*The usual stampede to be first off.* MARK *comes sidling through with his light bag, tough and independent. He stops near where the* GIRLS *are.* PASSENGERS *are getting out their passports.* MARK *pats his pocket confidently. He frowns. He pats another pocket. He looks on the floor. He bends and starts to crawl between legs. The crowd begins to move forward.* MARK *rises and tries to prevent them.*

MARK: Excuse me, but I wonder if by any chance, someone's picked up the wrong passport. If you wouldn't mind –

> *They brush past him impatiently. He plunges about wildly.*

OFFICER: Look in your bag, sir.

MARK: I know it isn't in my bag. Someone's obviously taken it –

OFFICER: I doubt that, sir. Try –

MARK (*furious*): You know what a passport's worth on the black market? A valid Royal Britannic Majestic passport? On the black market in Naples? A hundred pounds. At least.

OFFICER: This is France.

MARK: I don't have the latest figures for France. I can see myself stuck on this boat for the rest of my life going backwards and forwards, backwards and forwards –

OFFICER: I can't see that happening.

MARK: I can see it happening. I can see it happening very easily. What do you think you're doing?

*He has spotted* JOANNA *feeling in the pocket flap of his bag which he has left, in his frenzy, on the floor. Most of the* PASSENGERS *have now leaked off, but the last remnants, including several of the* GIRLS, *are still jostling down the narrow stairs.*

MARK: You leave something for two seconds and –

JOANNA *silences him by holding up the missing passport.*

MARK (*takes the passport with consummate grudgingness*): Thank you.

JOANNA: You're welcome.

MARK (*unamused*): Ha!

*J*OANNA *turns to go.* MARK *snatches up his bag, which* JOANNA *has not refastened. His strap pulls out and all his stuff goes rolling down the stairs. He scrambles after it and stuffs it all into his sack, his back to us. He straightens up and we see (still from behind) him pat his pockets again with increasing desperation. In panic, he turns and there is the passport gripped firmly between his teeth. The* OFFICER *is watching him.* MARK *makes to speak – realizes where his passport is and, with a sheepish show of individuality, goes on his way.*


10. INT. *QUAY. CUSTOMS SHED. DAY.*
*A British passport bearing the name* MARK WALLACE *is stamped by a French* OFFICIAL. *It is removed and a passport bearing the name* MRS JOANNA WALLACE *is stamped.* JOANNA *is now included as she takes the passport. It is five years later. Behind* JOANNA *in the background we see an antique folding-topped M.G.*


10a. EXT. *QUAY. DAY.*
*They go to the car.* MARK *gets in and starts the engine.*

43

MARK: Hold your breath. We've got a long way to go.

*He eases out the clutch. The car doesn't move. It stalls. MARK can't start it again.*

MARK: What we need is a small push.

*They look at each other. JOANNA smiles. She stops smiling. She gets out and pushes. MARK revs importantly. The OFFICIAL watches. JOANNA looks at him appealingly, but he is carefully combing his bald head. The car catches and leaps forward with a jerk, almost flattening JOANNA on her face behind it. The car moves forward smartly out of the shed.*

*JOANNA scampers after the car.*

JOANNA: Oy!

*MARK makes a circle round the area and returns.*

JOANNA (*climbs aboard*): Remember me? Joanna?

*MARK looks worried, signals her to be quiet.*

JOANNA: What's the matter?
MARK: That donk. Hear it?
JOANNA: Donk? What kind of donk?
MARK: A medium-sized slightly unhealthy donk. A donk.
JOANNA: I can't hear anything. All I care about is, I've got you to myself for two whole weeks. Donk or no donk.
MARK: Hell, I'm not away much.
JOANNA: You're not away much at all. You're just away too much.

*They have made another trial circuit. MARK nods at JOANNA, it's all right. He waves to the bald OFFICIAL and away they go.*

11. EXT. *THE ROAD (MERCEDES). DAY.*
*We have cut as the M.G. changes gear and now the Mercedes charges away. MARK and JOANNA fasten their seat belts.*

MARK: My father's almost completely bald.
JOANNA: He's older than you.
MARK: That's true. But I'm catching up. So is Hal Van Benius. Bald.

44

JOANNA: Who cares about Hal Van Benius? You're not related.
MARK: I don't like the idea of working with a man who reminds me of – (*examines his hairline anxiously in the mirror*) – the inevitable.
JOANNA: The inevitable may never happen.
MARK: Of course it'll happen if it's inevitable. It'll happen. It's inevitable.

> JOANNA *makes a face. How can you argue?*

MARK: Anyway, you don't want to go, do you?
JOANNA: Go bald?
MARK (*unamused*): Ha! Go to the States. (*Explains impatiently*) If I work with Hal on this project, it means at least two years in the States.
JOANNA: Goody. (*Looks at his suspicious face*) Not goody?
MARK: You don't really want to go.
JOANNA: Look, if you want to go to the States, I want to go to the States. If you don't want to go to the States – (*thinks*) – I want to go to the States. Let's go to the States!
MARK: We can't go to the States. I haven't been offered the commission yet. How can we go to the States?

> JOANNA *looks at him thoughtfully. She screams.*

12. EXT. *FERRY QUAY. FRANCE. DAY.*
MARK *at first sight seems to be hitch-hiking along the open road.*

JOANNA (*over this*): You were just a happy barefoot boy before you met me, weren't you? Swinging along without a care in the world!

> *It looks like it, until he winces and bends to ease his boot, blowing out his cheeks with exhaustion, as if he has walked a hundred miles. We now ease back, as he removes his boot, to disclose that he is still directly underneath the ferryboat. He has walked a hundred yards. He puts his boot on a stack of crates and rests his foot on a bollard. Cars go by, to which he waves a hopeful thumb. They ignore him. The last is a Mini-bus with all the GIRLS in it, PAT WAIN-WRIGHT at the wheel. The GIRLS look tempting, but prove unhelpful.*

45

JOANNA (*over this*): You didn't want anything from anyone, did you?
MARK (*over*): Nothing permanent.

## 12a. INT. *MERCEDES. DAY.*
JOANNA: Thanks.

## 12b. *RESUME MARK.*
*He dreams for a moment of the* GIRLS *and then reaches for his boot. He looks. The stack of crates has gone. He looks round. He looks up. The whole bundle of crates is swinging high above his head. He raises a protesting yell and the boot falls off the top of the crates and he catches it out of sheer surprise.*
MARK: Thanks.

## 13. EXT. *THE M.G. THE ROAD. DAY.*
JOANNA *is driving. A broad smile on her face.*

JOANNA (*over, half-humorously*): When did it all start to go wrong? When did we have our first – you know –
MARK (*over*): Our first you know –
JOANNA (*over*): Was it in the M.G.? (*Pause*) Our first – bust up.
MARK (*over*): I thought we were quite happy in the M.G.
JOANNA (*over*): I thought we were quite happy in the M.G.

*Voice over ends.*

## 13a. EXT. *M.G. DAY.*
JOANNA: This is what I call real independence, don't you?
MARK: I can still hear that damned donk. Hear that? Donk – donk –
JOANNA (*blithely*): It's in the engine.
MARK: Right!

## 13b. *THE M.G. DRIVES ON TO A FERRY BOAT.*
*A broad placid river in mid-France with poplars growing, and reflected Sisley-style in the water. The ferry boat goes in an unhurried fashion across. An impression of all the time in the world.*

## 13c. EXT. *M.G. DAY.*

JOANNA (*deep breath*): Do you realize that this is the first afternoon I've spent in natural light for over a year? By the time I get home from work, it's pitch black.

MARK: Originally, you said you liked basements.

JOANNA: Originally I liked basements.

MARK: I think we were damn lucky to get the place frankly.

JOANNA: Look, I think we were damn lucky to get the place frankly. And I think one day we'll be damn lucky to get out of it frankly.

*He shakes his head and puts his arm round her.*

MARK: If you want to live in one half of a suburban shoebox like your parents do, you married the wrong man.

JOANNA: I don't want to live in one half of a suburban shoebox –

*She kisses him.*

JOANNA: – and I married the wrong man.

## 13d. INT. *THE MERCEDES. DAY.*

MARK: Do you want a divorce?

*There is a sudden change in temperature.* MARK *changes expression.* JOANNA *looks irritated.*

MARK: Why do we keep on with this farce? Is it bloody worth it? Is it?

JOANNA (*yells at him*): No, it isn't!

MARK: It was your idea. You wanted it.

JOANNA: And I've got it! (*Pause*) Yes – it is worth it. Sometimes.

*He smiles at her. She loves him.*

JOANNA: Only not now.

*He stops smiling. She doesn't love him.*

MARK: I really don't know what you ever saw in me in the first place.

JOANNA: I really can't remember. (*Pause – looks at him*) You had hair in those days, of course.

MARK *looks in the driving mirror in some alarm. He gives* JOANNA *a jaundiced look. She smiles blandly.*

MARK: So did you.

JOANNA*'s smile vanishes.*

13e. *THE M.G. DRIVES OFF THE FERRY BOAT.*

13f. INT. *M.G. DAY.*

MARK: Look – if you want big houses and fast cars and hot and cold running servants –

JOANNA: Who wants that?

MARK: I know what you want. You want big houses and fast cars –

JOANNA: You're right – there is a donk.

MARK: There is? I thought there was.

*He cocks his head.*

JOANNA: Definitely. (*Taps his head*) In there. Donk, donk, donk. There's something loose. No question.

MARK: If there is, you've loosened it.

*A donk from the engine.*

MARK: Joanna, keep out of the lower gears.

JOANNA: You keep out of the lower gears.

*She takes her hands off the wheel and offers him the driving seat.*

MARK: Joanna – you –

JOANNA: Go on!

*She climbs across him and he takes over the controls just in time.*

MARK: You're crazy.

*The M.G. goes away from us with* MARK *shaking his head at* JOANNA *who smiles brightly at him and leans back, tipping her seat so that she almost falls into the back.*

MARK: See? No donk, if you're careful.

MARK (*over*): I don't think we had any kind of real you know in the M.G.  Bust up.

*Suddenly there is a terrible clank and the M.G., which has been accelerating away, slows and lurches into the side. JOANNA tries to keep a straight face as MARK glares at the world and at her. They stare at each other.*

MARK (*quite amiable ferocity*): Oh, shut up ...

## 14. EXT. *THE ROAD. THE M.G. DAY.*

*A car flashes by and a pair of legs hurriedly retract under the beached M.G.*

MARK *is underneath and it is very dark. We dimly see his black face and the dripping, oily underbelly of the M.G.*

MARK: I hate this – can't see a – oil in my eye now – I could happily –

JOANNA (*calls*): How is it down there?

MARK: Pitch black. This stinking exhaust pipe is so rusty I could – if I could just see –

*Cut to JOANNA, sitting calmly in the front seat peeling hard-boiled eggs.*

JOANNA: It is difficult trying to do things in the dark, isn't it?

MARK's *head comes out.*

MARK: We can not afford a new flat.

*A car hoots. The head goes in. And comes out again.*

MARK: On the present budget we can't even afford a new exhaust pipe.

JOANNA: You really ought to try avoiding the lower gears.

MARK: Why don't you put a very British sock in it?

*He looks up at JOANNA's smiling face.*

JOANNA: Why don't you put a hard-boiled egg in it?

*She pops it into his mouth. He disappears. There is a grinding noise.*

MARK (*calls*): That's fixed it.

*He comes out from under.*

JOANNA: Do you mean (*brightly*) that's fixed it? Or (*gloomily*) that's fixed it?

MARK (*getting into the car*): Ask me in an hour's time.

## 15. EXT. *ROAD. DAY.*

MARK, *the student, is sitting in the back of a tractor-pulled farm cart loaded with turnips. The* DRIVER *sits ahead, hugely inflated in wind-filled oilskins.*

*The Mini-bus comes sweeping past them (the* GIRLS *have had lunch along the way) and the heads all turn and smile at* MARK.

PAT WAINWRIGHT *takes her eye off the road and it is for a second too long. The Mini-bus goes into a long, dramatic skid and slithers into the ditch.*

*It is not serious – as we see from* MARK'S *p.o.v. as the tractor comes level and the* GIRLS *spill out. The tractor* DRIVER, *on a wink from* MARK, *drives straight past.*

*The* GIRLS *call 'oy' and beg for help with hand signals.*

MARK *looks down on them superbly. He's not helping. The* GIRLS *look beseechingly. He's helping. He winks at the* DRIVER.

## 16. EXT. *THE SAME. DAY.*

*The Mini-bus comes jerking out of the ditch, with* MARK *at the wheel – a tow rope connects him with the tractor. The Mini-bus gains the road with its engine running, none the worse. The* GIRLS *scamper into it out of the wet, avoiding passing cars.*

## 17. EXT. *THE MINI-BUS. THE ROAD. DAY.*

*The bus with* MARK *at the wheel moving briskly along. The mouths of the* GIRLS *can be seen moving in unison – though no sound is heard.*

MARK *looks quizzical.*

## 18. INT. *THE MINI-BUS. DAY.*

*The* GIRLS *are singing their heads off. Bach. They are a choir.*

PAT WAINWRIGHT *is sitting near* MARK, *breathing song down his neck.*

*The Cantata ends.* PAT *sighs and wriggles.*

JACKIE: What's wrong with you?

PAT: Nothing. Everything. I don't think travel agrees with me.

    *She scratches vigorously.*

JACKIE: I hope it isn't measles.

    *She and* MARK *exchange warm smiles.*

PAT: I've had measles, clever. No, it must be something else –

    MARK *smiles and then has to brake hurriedly.*

## 19. EXT. *ENTRANCE TO FARMYARD. DAY.*

*A clutch of chickens has strayed on to the road. The faces of the Mini-bus occupants stare down at them.* MARK *looks at the chickens and then at* PAT. *The chickens cluck.* PAT's *face goes pink with horror. She begins to scratch convulsively.*

## 20. INT. *CLINIC. ABBEVILLE. NIGHT.*

PAT *standing there. And another* GIRL. *And a third* GIRL. *All very long-faced. And spotty.*

DOCTOR's *voice*: Chickenpox. No question.

## 21. INT. *SMALL HOTEL. ABBEVILLE. NIGHT.*

JACKIE: That's messed everything up. But completely.

    *Five of the* GIRLS *and* MARK *are having a rather sketchy supper, with a soup tureen as the centre-piece.*

MARK: Messed what up but completely? I mean ... what're you on exactly?

JACKIE: We're supposed to be going on holiday together and then on to the Music Festival at Menton. Middle of the month. What we do now, I don't know.

SALLY: Golly, nor do I.

    *She scratches her head ruefully. She scratches her ear. She scratches.*

SALLY: Oh no!

JACKIE: And then there were four.

MARK *and she are isolated in a tight two-shot.*

JACKIE: Only one thing to do, I s'pose, and that's see who's left in the morning.

MARK: Good plan.

## 22. INT. *LOBBY. SAME HOTEL. DAY.*

MARK *comes down the narrow stairs and looks across the room. There, with an expression which can only be called frankly triumphant, sits* JACKIE, *alone.*

MARK: Well, well, well.

JACKIE: How are you this morning?

MARK: I'm very well. How are you?

JACKIE: Very well indeed.

MARK: And – um – the others?

JACKIE (*grins*): I'm afraid it's been a night full of casualties.

MARK: I am sorry.

JACKIE: I think we should leave them the Mini-bus and press on. Does that appeal to you?

MARK: How can you be so callous? When do we leave?

> MARK *has sat down and now raises his coffee cup to* JACKIE.

JOANNA (*answers his question o.s.*): Whenever you're ready!

> MARK *and* JACKIE *turn to see a radiant* JOANNA *approaching them.*

JACKIE: Joanna, I thought you'd gone to the doctor!

JOANNA: I drove the others. There's nothing wrong with me.

MARK: Are you positive?

JACKIE: That feeling can be very deceptive.

MARK: Right. The calm before the spots.

JOANNA: I had chickenpox when I was twelve. Look.

> *She points to a tiny pit in her forehead.*

JOANNA: I scratched.

> *She grins at both of them.*

JACKIE: We're not taking the bus. We're leaving that for the others. When they're better. We thought we'd hitch –

JOANNA: I love hitch-hiking! (*She smiles happily*) I won't be in the way, will I?
MARK: What gave you that idea?

> *He and* JACKIE *watch* JOANNA *bleakly as* JOANNA *skips over to the map on the wall.*

JOANNA: Where do you think we'll get to by tonight?
> *She points well down the map, almost as far as Lyon, and turns questioningly to* MARK. *He goes and points somewhere still north of Paris.*

JOANNA: Oh we can do much better than that, can't we Jacqueline?
MARK: Can we, Jacqueline?

> *But* JACKIE *is not attending. She is trying to reach an irritating place which is itching between her shoulder blades. The other two turn and watch with interest her extravagant contortions. She stops and looks at them with sudden realization. She straightens up and attempts to look casual.*

JOANNA: JACKIE! (*She clucks like a chicken*) Puck-puck-puck-pooh!

> JACKIE *raises two fingers to her temples and mock shoots herself through the head.*

## 23. EXT. *ROAD NEAR AQUEDUCT. COUNTRY. DAY.*
JOANNA *hiking happily along, eyes everywhere.* MARK *stumbles moodily behind her.* JOANNA *sees some lambs in the fields and points them out to* MARK. *He nods unenthusiastically.*
JOANNA: Lambs!
MARK: I guessed.
JOANNA: Aren't they sweet?

> *He nods. They walk on.*

JOANNA: Isn't it a shame about Jacqueline?
MARK: Isn't it?

> *They march on.*

JOANNA: I expect you'd have preferred it if I'd been the one who got chickenpox.

*A good pause.*

*They hitch a passing lorry without success.* MARK *makes a face.*

JOANNA: You don't have to stay with me, you know.

MARK (*imitating Bogart*): Sweetheart, let's get this quite straight. I have no intention whatever of staying with you. I don't know what your plans are, but I have a schedule. I am not – whatever you may be – on holiday.

JOANNA: I understand.

MARK: I'm in Europe strictly for the buildings. Anything else is entirely by the way. I don't have a minute to waste.

JOANNA *nods like a rebuked younger sister. They walk on.*

MARK: My time is organized.

JOANNA: You have a schedule.

MARK: But a tight schedule.

*She nods again. She looks at him. She walks on. She looks.*

JOANNA: Did you pick up your passport when you left the hotel this morning?

MARK *stops as if shot. He starts the patting routine.* JOANNA *walks on.* MARK *runs across the road and gesticulates madly in front of the oncoming saloon, which stops reluctantly.* MARK *scrambles in, yelling incoherently.*

MARK'S P.O.V. *He hears a shout –*

JOANNA: Mark –

*And sees her holding up the missing passport. He is already in the car, looking out through the back window. The* DRIVER *starts moving, but* MARK *is already opening the far door and scrambling out. The car moves off with both back doors open.*

*He dives across the road and reaches* JOANNA, *furious. He snatches the passport from her hand. Her look is irresistible. He begins to see the humour and can't hold on any longer.*

MARK: If there's one thing I really despise, it's an indispensable woman.

*He smiles and starts walking along really with her, pointing out a roof on a barn and, as they go from us, making some comment on its structure.*

## 24. EXT. *SENLIS CATHEDRAL. DAY.*
MARK *photographing the great tympanum. He shoots first from one angle and then from another. Carefully. Accurately.*

MARK (*over this*): No one knows the names of the men who made it.

*She is standing looking up at it. He keeps shooting.*

MARK: To make something as exquisite as this and not want to leave your stupid name all over it –

JOANNA: Would you want to?

MARK: All you hear nowadays is about people making names. Not things.

*He lifts the camera for another shot. JOANNA has wandered over so that she is right in line for the picture. She assumes he's seen where she is and smiles, supposing he wants her picture. MARK frowns and gestures her to a place to one side. She goes there and arranges herself – thinking this is where he wants to shoot her. But when he clicks the camera, it is pointing at where she was before, at a leering gargoyle. He turns to her and lowers the camera.*

MARK: Oh! I'm sorry! Did you want me to take your picture?

JOANNA: No, no, no, no.

MARK (*busily packing up*): Only this is a three-dimensional camera. It's really for taking three-dimensional subjects.

JOANNA: I'm three-dimensional as a matter of fact.

MARK (*fastening the case*): It's basically for buildings.

JOANNA: Oh well, I'm not a building!

## 25. EXT. *STREET. MARKET. SENLIS. DAY.*
JOANNA *and* MARK *appear at the head of the street.* JOANNA *looks*

*terribly excited and they come down towards the rows of stalls brilliant with fresh vegetables, flowers, etc. We track with them until we lose them behind a stall. We track on quickly and pick them up coming out of the bottom of the street, their arms full of little paper bags and both of them armed with 'baguettes', the slim, long, crisp bread that's best for picnics.*

JOANNA: We won't have to waste a minute stopping for lunch!

> *She breaks off a piece of bread and hands it to him, with a tomato. A small van hoots them from behind. They part to let it through and hitch it as they do so.*

## 26. EXT. *THE VAN. COUNTRY. DAY.*

JOANNA *and* MARK *crouch in the open back of the van among a mass of scaffolding shackles.* MARK *puts the tomato in his mouth and offers* JOANNA *a piece of cheese from one of his bags.*

MARK: The trouble with American women is, they want to label you. Put you in a pigeon-hole. What they don't realize is, the only thing that really fits in a pigeon-hole is a pigeon.

## 27. EXT. *THE ROAD. DAY.*

JOANNA *puts the cheese in her mouth. But we pull back to disclose that they are now hiking along the main road again. The little van turns up a lane towards a building site. The dialogue and the 'picnic action' continue throughout this sequence without allowing for the breaks in scenic background.*

MARK: Marriage is all they ever think about. I have no intention of marrying for at least forty years.

> JOANNA *hands him an apple from one of her bags. He looks at it suspiciously. She thumbs an approaching vehicle ...*

## 28. INT. *FURNITURE LORRY. DAY.*

MARK *bites into the apple.*

MARK: Not that I have anything against sex.

> JOANNA *looks at him. They are sitting opposite each other in comfortable armchairs, with a standard lamp at* MARK's *elbow and a birdcage in the background.*

MARK: It's contracts I don't go for. Promises of long service and good conduct. Are you a virgin?

JOANNA: I –

MARK: Thought you were. I have a built-in virgin-detector.

JOANNA: Congratulations.

MARK: I was two years at the University of Chicago.

JOANNA: Studying virgin-detection?

*He hands her a salami sandwich.*

MARK: Only at night school.

## 29. INT. *CITROEN* (*2 CV*). *DAY*.

JOANNA *bites into the salami sandwich and we ease back to show that they are now crushed together in the back of the tiny car which is seesawing uphill in the classic* deux chevaux *style, driven by a large, beret-wearing* PEASANT.

MARK: Architecture during the day. You know, I always thought American women would be different. I thought America had broken through the inhibitions barrier, and it was all one long sex-fest.

JOANNA: No?

MARK: But no, but no. The nicely brought up American girl may play it cool and modern, but what she wants is what her grandmother wanted –

JOANNA *produces a banana and offers it to* MARK.

## 30. EXT. *ROADSIDE. DAY.*

*The banana skin flung into the ditch.*

MARK (*over*): Your head stuffed and mounted on the living-room wall!

MARK *and* JOANNA *are hitching along the roadside again.*

MARK: And if you don't want it that way, take your loving self elsewhere – I'm speaking quite generally, of course.

JOANNA: Of course. Who was she?

MARK: Whaddya mean?

*He grins and hands her a peach.*

## 31. INT. *CAB. GIANT ARTICULATED LORRY. DAY.*
JOANNA *bites the peach.*

MARK: Her name was Cathy Seligman, if you must know.

> JOANNA *offers the* DRIVER *some grapes off the bunch. He smiles at her agreeably and takes some.*
>
> *The lorry has eased away from us somewhat and the cab slides forward out of shot.*

## 32. EXT. *THE ROAD. DAY.*
*The articulated lorry moves forward to clear the frame.*

MARK (O.S.): Selfish, grasping, Philistine, materialistic, stubborn, opinionated – I was crazy about her.

> *The lorry clears the frame and we pick up the car which appears to follow it (without a cut). It is a Ford station wagon with four* ADULTS *and a* CHILD *in it. Tags hang from the luggage on the roof.*

## 32a. EXT. *THE NAME HOWARD MAXWELL MANCHESTER IS ON THEM.*
CATHY *is looking out of the window.*

MARK (*as we hold on* CATHY): Mrs Howard Maxwell Manchester, no less. Luckily for you, you'll never be called upon to spend too much time in her company.

> CATHY *is very pretty and doesn't look quite as vampirish as* MARK'*s young tongue suggested. It is some three years later and the* MANCHESTERS *and the* WALLACES *are making a joint expedition, as we shall shortly see.*

## 33. INT. *THE FORD. DAY.*
*Roars of laughter! Such a happy party!*

MARK: I always thought you two ought to meet.
CATHY: There's only one drawback, Howard said, we'll have to go to Greece! Remember saying that, Howie?
HOWARD: Yes.

*There is a fly buzzing on the windscreen and* CATHY *has been flapping at it ineffectually.* HOWARD'S *hand comes into shot with an aerosol spray in it. Fwhoosh! End of fly.*

CATHY: Drawback! Of course I absolutely flipped!

MARK *and* JOANNA *are sitting in the back, with luggage, a cot, other stuff all piled in the compartment behind them.* RUTH'S *toy box keeps slipping off into the back of* MARK'S *neck.*

CATHY: Naturally the first thing we thought of landing in England, was getting in touch with you. Mind you, I never thought you newly-weds (MARK *winces*) would want to travel with us ancients!

MARK (*big joke*): We don't care who we go with, Cathy, frankly.

CATHY: I'd guessed that!

*A pair of legs comes up between* CATHY *and* HOWARD. RUTH *is coming up from the floor where her two teddy bears and three dolls are having a party.*

RUTH: Mommy, do snakes have nipples?

CATHY: No, Ruthie, they don't. Do they, Howie?

HOWARD: No. They don't.

CATHY: Ruthie is hooked on nature. It's so wonderful you two kids were free to come with us. I just know we're all going to be terribly terrific friends!

*She leans over and smiles very warmly at both* MARK *and* JOANNA.

CATHY: Of course, Joanna, you know Mark used to be my favourite beau.

MARK: Second favourite.

CATHY: Favourite favourite. That was before you came on the scenario, Howie.

HOWARD: Of course.

RUTH: Why don't they?

HOWARD: Why don't who what?

RUTH: Snakes have nipples.

HOWARD: Because they lay eggs. Cathy, did we pack the anti-snake serum?

CATHY: Mark, do you remember David Lewinsohn? He's turned into a very fine physician in New York City. And he gave Howard a course in how to treat snake-bite. How to inject serum subcutaneously and all that. We've invested over sixty dollars in anti-snake equipment.

MARK: Wow! I sure hope someone gets bitten.

*The speedometer turns to another mile.*

HOWARD *brakes sharply and the travelling cot bumps* MARK *sharply on the head.* HOWARD *looks at his watch, then at the distance gauge.*

HOWARD: That's my hundred exactly. Now let me see –

*He takes out a notebook from the glove compartment.* MARK *rubs his head.*

HOWARD: Mark, it's you to drive – and – oh, we change places, that's all there is to it.


## 33a. EXT. *ROAD. DAY.*

*He gets out of the car and* MARK *and he change places,* MARK *to drive. The car starts off again.*


## 33b. INT. *FORD. DAY.*

RUTH: I'm hungry.

JOANNA: I think Howard's wonderful the way he organizes everything.

CATHY: He's not an efficiency consultant for nothing, are you, sweetness?

MARK: If he were, he wouldn't be married to you, honey.

CATHY: Still a cat, Wallace, aren't you? Grrrr!

RUTH: I'm hungry!

HOWARD (*looks at watch*): We stop for lunch in exactly – nineteen and a half minutes. Pass me the guide book, sugar.

RUTH: I want to eat something now!

RUTH *is three and a half and a very* expressive *child.*

CATHY *has opened the second compartment and revealed a shelf of guide books. She hands the Michelin to* HOWARD.

CATHY: If you want to ruin your lunch, Ruthiebelle, you can.

*She presses a button and a miniature larder is opened to our eyes. Fruit, biscuits, cheese, etc.*

HOWARD: We believe in leaving things to Ruthie's own free decision.

RUTH (*to* MARK): Does that key make the car go?

MARK: Sort of.

*RUTH eyes the ignition. MARK eyes RUTH. RUTH looks at him very long and hard and then turns and pinches her mother with ferocity.*

CATHY: Ruthie, that hurt Mommy! Howie, did you see that? She pinched me.

HOWARD: She probably thinks you're excluding her, honey-bunch. She needs reassuring.

CATHY: If she does it again, I'm going to need hospitalization.

*RUTH starts to scream.*

HOWARD: Well, we're covered. (*To* JOANNA) Have you ever been in analysis?

JOANNA: No!

HOWARD: It can be very worthwhile.

JOANNA (*seeing* RUTH *at* CATHY *again*): Would you like me to tell you a story, Ruth?

*RUTH nods and starts to climb over on to the back seat to JOANNA. CATHY smiles at MARK rather intimately.*

CATHY: Well, well, well. Quite like old times, Mr Wallace!

34. EXT. *RESTAURANT. DAY.*
*The Ford comes into the car-park and stops, with rather a jolt. The luggage falls forward inside on to HOWARD and JOANNA.*

*MARK gets out and opens HOWARD's door. A ball rolls out, some blankets, stuff like that. And HOWARD.*

HOWARD: I see what you mean about readjusting the luggage, Marcus.

MARK: Thought you might, Howie.

*The car is parked in bright sunlight.*

CATHY (*getting out*): Wow, that's a sun now!

HOWARD: Getting way down south, honah!

*He starts adjusting ropes – lugging things out of the back.*

RUTH: I'm hungry!

*Speeded-up action: they all immediately restore luggage inside, shut doors, lock the car, pick up* RUTH *and scamper into the restaurant.*

## 35. INT. *THE RESTAURANT. DAY.*

*Speeded-up action continued: a table is laid, cushions are brought, food is ordered, water is poured, waiters dash back and forth, napkins are adjusted, food is brought and served.*

*The action returns to normal speed as* CATHY *puts food in a spoon for* RUTH *and gives it to her.*

RUTH: I don't want anything to eat.

HOWARD: I think maybe she's going to be a little late fixating. She felt we hurried her. Let's all relax. Marcus – I've been meaning to say about expenses. I think I've come up with a formula. If you're agreeable, we'll call Ruthie a half, in which event we can most efficaciously divide everything into nine parts, and split them in the ratio of five to four.

*During this* RUTH *ostentatiously refuses to eat, pressing her lips together. The rest of them eat guiltily.*

## 36. EXT. *THE ROAD. DAY.*

*The M.G. bowls past the restaurant going very well.*

MARK: I (*smiles*) fixed it!

JOANNA *smiles at him. She looks at the restaurant where the Ford turned in and makes a face.*

MARK: I once ate with some friends there.

JOANNA (*innocently*): Oh, really? I must say, it's nice to own our own wheels, don't you think?

MARK: I do think. (*Listens for donk*) I think I think.

## 37. INT. *THE RESTAURANT. DAY.*

*The bill has been brought and* HOWARD *is doing the necessary division.* RUTH *still sits there. She snatches the pencil out of* HOWARD'*s hand and starts to draw on the tablecloth.* CATHY *goes to stop her, but* HOWARD *signals her to leave* RUTH *to it. He takes a pen from his pocket and goes on working.*

HOWARD: I think that's the final breakdown on the morning's figures, Marcus, if you'd care to check.

MARK: I believe you.

HOWARD: Well, shall we go?

> *They get up.* HOWARD *starts apologetically bribing the* WAITER *over the tablecloth.* RUTHIE *has drawn a house on it.*

RUTH: You don't like my house, do you?

MARK: It's very handsome. Split level. Market at about twenty-five thousand. I like it a lot.

CATHY: It's beautiful, Ruthiebelle! Come on, sweetheart.

> *They get up to go.*

RUTH: I want to take my house with me.

HOWARD: She's feeling insecure. Very natural.

CATHY: Come on, sweetness.

RUTH: I WANT TO TAKE MY HOUSE WITH ME!

> *She gives the tablecloth a great pull; the wine spills, the water spills and runs in a great river on to* JOANNA'*s lap as she gets up.* JOANNA, *infuriated, slaps the child's hand almost before she knows what she's done. There is a stunned silence.* HOWARD *rubs his neck. He consults the ceiling. He controls himself.*

RUTH: I WANT IT!

CATHY: Ruthie, this time I have to say no. And I mean no. Now no.

## 38. EXT. *THE RESTAURANT. DAY.*

*They come out.* RUTH *is trailing the tablecloth.*

HOWARD: It's very reassuring at times to retain a certain flexibility of attitude.

*JOANNA walks out alone. HOWARD is with RUTH (the last line being addressed to CATHY over his shoulder). CATHY is with MARK.*

CATHY: Howard has a tremendously mature quality, Marcus, that's what I love about him. He has quiet assurance. Don't you think he has quiet assurance?

MARK: Very quiet assurance.

*HOWARD has reached the car and unlocks the door. The handle is hot. The car has stood in the mid-day sun for far too long.*

CATHY: He's the husband type. You were always the lover type. I guess basically you still are –

MARK: Joanna and I have been married for two years.

CATHY: But your relationship is basically volatile. Anyone can see that.

*HOWARD is busy reloading the car, altering the position of the cases on the roof. He puts the cot right on top now and readjusts the ropes. JOANNA helps, dutifully. RUTH plays in the dust.*

HOWARD: Joanna, I don't want you to feel badly about what happened just now.

JOANNA (*forgiving*): Oh it doesn't matter!

HOWARD: I think it does matter, Joanna. Would you mind?

*He dumps a large suitcase in her arms.*

HOWARD: You resent Ruth, don't you, Joanna?

JOANNA: Listen, a little spilt wine –

HOWARD: You misunderstand me. You resent her because she represents the child you want to have.

*JOANNA looks at RUTH, busy pulling at one of the rubber straps, stretching it further and further.*

HOWARD: Ruthie, may I have that now, honey?

*RUTH lets go as her father turns and the rubber strap springs back and catches him on the head.*

64

## 39. INT. *THE CAR. DAY.*

HOWARD *has finished rubbing his head and arranging the luggage.*

HOWARD: Everybody in! We're seventeen minutes behind schedule. Mark, you have fifty-three kilometres still to run. O.K.?

*They start to get into the car. The seats are very hot.*

RUTH: It's hot.

CATHY: Sweetheart, I hate to say it but we should've left the car under the sun-shelter, Howie.

HOWARD: I know, sugarbush.

*They go through the usual pantomime of people sitting in a hot car. When MARK takes the wheel it almost sears his hands off.*

HOWARD: Let's move it, Marcus, eh?

MARK *starts the car and steers it – one hand then the other – out into the road.*


## 39a. INT. *MOVING FORD. DAY.*

RUTH: Mommy.

CATHY: What is it, candyface?

RUTH: I'm hungry.


## 39b. EXT. *THE ROAD. DAY.*

*The M.G. rolling along. A lyrical feeling to the drive. They are both very happy.* JOANNA *has on* MARK'S *motoring jacket and is deep in it with a knitted cap on her head, sitting close to* MARK. *They speak with long pauses: in no hurry.*

MARK: Better look for a camping ground soon.

JOANNA: Mmmm.

MARK: I don't know about you, but I've got an appetite.

JOANNA: So've I.

MARK: Yes?

JOANNA: Mmm. And I'm hungry as well.

*He looks down at her and kisses her. She comes even closer to him.*

MARK: A few more miles – all right?

C 65

*She nods. They have come to a sharpish corner.* MARK *works on the wheel, but there is no response. The M.G. cruises serenely over the verge, through a half-open gate, down a dusty path to the edge of a small, beautiful river, through a bush or two and stops among the willows and reeds.*

JOANNA (*she has closed her eyes but now opens them*): Changed your mind?

MARK: Yes.

*Near by, on the far side of the river, a few sheep are grazing. They bleat gently.* MARK *and* JOANNA *exchange looks.*

## 40. EXT. *THE ROAD. DAY.*

MARK *and* JOANNA, *on foot, finishing their hitch-hike picnic. Their hitching luck has changed and they are finding it hard going.* MARK *screws up one of the remaining picnic bags and throws it furiously after a departing car. He sits down and eases his boot.* JOANNA *contemplates him patiently.*

MARK: Oh it's all very funny, isn't it? But I happen to have a schedule. The trouble is there's two of us. That's the basis of the whole trouble.

JOANNA *nods slowly.*

*Another car flashes past.*

MARK (*rages again*): If I ever have a car, I'm never going to pass up a single hitch-hiker as long as I live.

*A white Mercedes flashes past, cutting off the roadside figures from our view for a moment. When they come into clear shot again, we see that they are now a pair of German* STUDENTS *with ponderous rucksacks, encouraging flags and innocent faces. They watch balefully as the Mercedes flashes away.*

## 41. EXT. *THE MERCEDES. ROAD. DAY.*

MARK's *expression is of amused contempt as they fizz past.*

JOANNA: Must we dice with death?

*They have been cutting in and out.* MARK *now brakes sharply.
Freeze frame:* MARK *and* JOANNA *frozen with their faces right
against the windscreen.*

## 41a. EXT. *ROAD & MERCEDES. DAY.*
*Action restarts: the Mercedes in the shadow of a large, peaceful wood.*

JOANNA (*easing back from windscreen*): Since when does this car
have only two speeds – a hundred and ten miles an hour and
stop?

MARK: I'll tell you what. You drive.

JOANNA (*opens her door*): I'll tell you what. I'll walk.

*She gets out of the car.* MARK *comes up level with her.*

MARK: O.K. Walk. (*He speaks coaxingly.*) Come on, Jo. Don't be
silly.

JOANNA: You'd have been much better off on your own,
wouldn't you?

MARK: Not again. Look, Joanna –

JOANNA: You want to get on, I know. Maurice's waiting.

MARK: Let him wait.

JOANNA: He's got you on a line. All he has to do is start reeling in
and –

*She jerks her arm and lurches away as if someone has suddenly
tugged a rope attached to her wrist.*

MARK: Will you shut the hell up about Maurice? If it weren't
for Maurice, do you know where we'd be?

JOANNA: Happy.

MARK: Broke.

JOANNA: Broke and happy.

MARK: Want to go back to living in a cellar? You hated it.

JOANNA: I loved it.

MARK: You hated it.

JOANNA: I hated it.

*They smile at each other. The row seems over. But it catches fire
again.*

JOANNA: I hate being at other people's beck and call, that's all. As soon as anyone becks or calls, I resent it, that's all.

MARK: So you run the show. You handle it. You worry about the house and the flat and Nanny and Mrs Rathbone –

JOANNA: I don't want any of them.

MARK: So? Am I the one who has crocodile travelling bags already?

JOANNA: Have your lousy crocodile-skin travelling bag. (*She hurls it at him*) I don't want it. I don't want anything.

MARK: Nothing makes a woman more bloody-minded than giving her everything she wants.

JOANNA: You don't give me everything I want. You give me everything you want to give me.

> MARK *holds out the bag.*

MARK: Joanna. Your bag.

> *She takes it, and walks a couple of steps back towards the car.*

MARK: Joanna. I love you.

JOANNA (*with her back still turned to him*): Come on, Maurice's waiting.

MARK (*watches her go back to the car and mutters softly to himself*): Bitch.

## 42. EXT. *THE ROAD. DAY.*

JOANNA *in* C.U. (*We are back with them hitch-hiking.*)

MARK (*Bogart again*): Look, kid, this is the kiss-off. We're not getting the breaks, that's all. So here's the thing – you take the low road and I'll take the high road and we'll see who's in where before who. O.K.?

> *He has now emerged from the ditch holding out her bag and dusting off his own.* JOANNA *nods with a kind of bright anguish.*

MARK: If we meet up some place – great. Otherwise, happy holidays!

> *He hands her her bag.*

MARK: No hard feelings but –

JOANNA: You have a schedule.
MARK: Right.

> *He grins and marches off, whistling.* JOANNA'*s face crumples for a moment in disappointment.* MARK *signals a truck. It ignores him.* JOANNA *presses her lips together and turns and raises a determinedly cheerful thumb.*

> *There is an instant squeal of breaks, as the first car she signals stops instantly. It is a red Alfa-Romeo.*

## 43. EXT. *THE ROAD. DAY.*

MARK, *on foot, watches miserably as a red Alfa-Romeo pulls away from the kerb and accelerates past him.* JOANNA'*s face peers out of the back, as she swings round to see the last of him. She waves gaily.* MARK *slings his bag on his back and toils on.*

## 44. EXT. *FILLING STATION. DAY.*

*The Ford, driven by* JOANNA, *pulls into a filling station. We see* HOWARD *get out his little book and start being very busy.*

*Speeded-up action: They all leap out and change places again. The* ATTENDANT *puts petrol in the car, checks oil and water, cleans the windscreen.* RUTH *also changes places in the rush and we note (without dwelling on it) that something has fallen from the car. The* ATTENDANT *signals them out into the main road and the car disappears into the distance. A wailing noise – unmistakably* RUTHIE!

*The car comes zooming back, zips into the service area; a door opens, the teddy bear is retrieved and the car is signalled out again by the* ATTENDANT *and disappears at full velocity.*

## 45. EXT. *ROAD WORKS. DAY.*

MARK *is trudging on grimly, hiking alone. He comes to where the road narrows and there is a large electric warning robot with stiff arms which wave up and down and have flashing red lights for 'hands'. There is also a flashing light on top of its 'head'. (This is a standard form of warning used in France.)*

*As* MARK *approaches this man-sized monster* JOANNA *steps out from behind it, mimicking exactly its jerky automatic movements, and making a weird honking noise at the same time.*

MARK: What happened to your silky friend in the Alfa-Romeo?

JOANNA: I explained that I was in love with you so he put me down.

> *He stares at her and then he realizes what she has said. She is indeed in love with him. Flattered and moved, he takes her in his arms. The same honking noise from behind them reveals a public service van whose way they are blocking. He takes her hand and they walk on.*

MARK (*a little hoarsely*): I warn you –

JOANNA: Well don't.


## 46. EXT. *SMALL VILLAGE. EVENING.*

*Start on: a group of sheep, packed rather tightly together. We ease back to reveal that they are in the back of a truck which has just pulled up in the square. Two heads – MARK's and JOANNA's – appear over the tail-board. They've got a lift at last. They climb out, MARK first. He helps JOANNA into his arms and so to the ground. They stretch.*

MARK: What would you say to a cup of coffee?

JOANNA: Baah!

> *He takes her arm and they cross – with a grateful wave to the DRIVER of the truck – towards a small café.*


## 47. EXT. *THE CAFÉ. NIGHT.*

*The cars are just switching on their lights. So are the shops their signs. And the cafés. The street lights come on.*

JOANNA *and* MARK *sit at a small table in front of a not very impressive café. She sits and stares at him. He stares at her. They lean forward and look at each other. The* PATRON *brings the coffee. They nod, but don't look up – stir their coffee, but don't look at it.*


## 48. INT. *THE CAFÉ. NIGHT.*

*A young* MAN *playing a pin table. The ball bounces from spring to spring and the lights flash up, mounting higher and higher. Through the*

*open door – we look from behind him outwards –* MARK *and* JOANNA
*can be seen looking at each other.* MARK *puts his hand on* JOANNA'*s.*
*They lean forward as if to kiss and then hold back.*

MARK *says something to* JOANNA. JOANNA *looks back and up at the*
*café – and nods.* MARK *smiles and gets up and comes into the café. He*
*goes up to the* PATRON.

MARK: Vous avez une chambre, Monsieur?

## 49. INT. *CAFÉ. NIGHT.*

MARK *and* JOANNA *have to go through the bar restaurant to reach the*
*narrow stairs which lead up to the bedrooms. A morose* MAN *and*
WOMAN *sit facing each other in desolate silence. As* MARK *and* JOANNA
*go by,* MARK *whispers:*

MARK: What kind of people just sit in a restaurant and don't say
one word to each other?

JOANNA: Married people?

 *He grins and takes her hand and they go upstairs.*

## 50. INT. *CAFÉ. NIGHT.*

*The pin table reaches a superb climax of flashing lights – the acme of pop*
*art electric pyrotechnics.*

## 51. INT. *CAFÉ. BEDROOM. NIGHT.*

MARK'*s hiking knapsack on a chair next to* JOANNA'*s bag.* MARK *and*
JOANNA *are in bed. They lie staring at the lights crossing the ceiling.*

MARK: You know, this is absolutely contrary to my principles.

JOANNA: Good. I wouldn't like to think it happened all the time.

MARK: I had absolutely no intention of sleeping in hotels.

JOANNA: You didn't?

MARK: Hell, what do you think I brought a sleeping bag for?

JOANNA: I hadn't seriously thought about it.

 *She is in a state of blissful, confused uncertainty.* MARK'*s*
 *matter-of-factness is so inappropriate that she almost finds it*
 *endearing. He senses her strangeness now and turns to her. He kisses*
 *her gently.*

71

MARK: Who are you?

JOANNA: Some girl.

> MARK *shakes his head. Rather too touchingly. For she has expressed very well what part of him thinks of her.*

## 51a. EXT. *SMALL ELEGANT HOTEL. DAY.*

MARK *and* JOANNA *are walking towards the parked Mercedes. A* BELLBOY *is carrying the luggage.*

MARK: Sleep well?

JOANNA (*yawning accusingly*): I think that room was on top of the plate-smashing annexe. I think my roughing-it days are over. Next time you must get Maurice to book us a room, if you can't remember yourself; preferably one with a carpet, and something else in the hot tap besides schwssssssglokglokgloksssss …

> MARK *hums an aggressive hum. He presses the button on the boot. The boot flies up, papers scatter everywhere. He leaps up and down.*

## 52. EXT. *THE ROAD. DAY.*

*The Mercedes passes the parked Ford.* JOANNA *is walking along the verge, abstracted, followed by a half-anxious, half-exasperated* MARK. HOWARD *is doing deep-breathing exercises.* CATHY *is looking at her face in the wing mirror and applying powder to her nose. What's it all about? It's all about* RUTH. *She is now seen sitting on her travelling pot – and taking her time about it.*

HOWARD *looks at his little book.*

HOWARD: When we're ready – it's Joanna in the hot seat and Catherine the great co-driver, check?

> JOANNA *looks at* MARK.

MARK: We have three weeks to go, so you may as well make the best of it.

JOANNA: Believe it or not, I am making the best of it.

MARK: You wanted to come.

HOWARD: O.K.?

> JOANNA *flashes a patently insincere smile, the insincerity of which only* MARK *fully appreciates.*

RUTH (*at* JOANNA): I don't want her to look at me.
CATHY (*comes up to* JOANNA): Joanna, may I say something?

> JOANNA *nods.*

CATHY: I know it may sound ridiculous to you. I know you love Ruthie, but she doesn't seem to realize. I don't think you're getting through to her. She's gotten the idea you're hostile [*she pronounces it 'host-ill'*] to her.

> JOANNA *blinks.*

CATHY: May I make a suggestion?
JOANNA: Please.
CATHY: Why don't you woo her a little?
JOANNA: Woo her ... ?
CATHY: That's right. Why don't you woo her a little?

> JOANNA *gulps and nods. During this,* HOWARD *has been tipping the pottie into the ditch and he is busy squirting it clean with an aerosol disinfectant. He straps the pot back on the roof and smiles encouragingly.*

HOWARD: O.K., let's get this show on the road.

## 53. INT. *THE FORD. DAY.*

CATHY *is consulting the guide book. She checks the symbols.*

CATHY: It has running hot and cold, bath, free garage, telephone and transistor radios are not allowed in the dining room.
HOWARD: Sounds minimal, but I'll buy it.
RUTH: I don't want to go to a hotel.
CATHY: Our own little home for the night. Of course you do, sweetness.
RUTH: I don't. I don't!

> *She is sitting in front, beside* JOANNA. *She turns and looks at the dashboard. The keys are dangling right in front of her. She snatches them out of the dashboard. The car slows down:* HOWARD *looks: and there is* RUTH *with the keys.*

## 53a. EXT. *ROAD. DAY.*

*The car rolls to a halt.*

HOWARD (*casually*): Ruthie, may I have the keys back now, please?

RUTH: No.

HOWARD: O.K. We'll just have to stay here all night. Is that what you want?

*A silence.*

RUTH: Yes.

*They sit.*

HOWARD: With nothing to eat.

*A silence.*

RUTH: I'm not hungry.

CATHY: She had a snack –

HOWARD: Cathy, please –

*They sit.* HOWARD *thinks. He thinks.*

HOWARD (*sharply*): Ruthie, will you please give me that KEY!

*He makes a dive, but* RUTH *is too quick. She throws the key out of the window into the verge.*

JOANNA *stares innocently ahead of her.*

## 54. EXT. *THE VERGE. NIGHT.*

*They are tramping the grass for the key.* HOWARD *has a flash-light.*

MARK: Don't you have a spare?

HOWARD: If I use the spare, we don't have a spare.

*They tramp.*

RUTH: Mommy, I'm so tired.

*She is sitting in the open door, her feet hanging down out of the car.* HOWARD *turns – very near the end of his tether – but restrains himself.*

MARK (*to* JOANNA, *quietly as they tramp away from the others*): You still want a child?

JOANNA: I want a child. I just don't want that child.

MARK: We agreed before we got married we weren't going to have any children.

JOANNA: And before we were married, we didn't.

HOWARD *has got hold of himself. He goes down on his knees in front of* RUTH.

HOWARD: Ruthie, you know that was kind of a very funny thing you did with the key. Fast thinking. Um, did you see where it landed?

RUTH: Yes.

HOWARD: Good girl! Where?

RUTH: I'm not going to tell you.

JOANNA *has wandered up from the other side and is suddenly right by* RUTH.

JOANNA: Tell Daddy at once!

RUTH *nearly jumps out of her skin and points before she can prevent herself to the key lying in the dirt by the roadside.*

HOWARD: Good girl!

JOANNA (*with a big smile*): I wooed her!

## 55. EXT. *THE RIVER BANK. DAY.*

*The M.G. is parked, covered with dew. It is early morning. Beautiful.* JOANNA *comes out of a tent, having packed up, and pulls a stopper out of the tent side. The tent immediately deflates. It is one of the special 'igloo' tents which don't need struts, functions on compressed air. The tent begins to wriggle.* MARK *is still inside.*

JOANNA: Your time's up, buddy!

MARK *crawls out from under.*

JOANNA: Breakfast is served.

*We ease back to show that* JOANNA *has set up the paraffin stove and made breakfast.*

## 55a. *THE SAME. DAY.*

MARK *sipping his tea.*

MARK: Boy, that's a good cup of tea.

JOANNA: It's coffee.

MARK: I knew it was a good cup of something.
JOANNA (*drily*): Baah!

## 55b. *THE SAME. DAY.*
MARK *in front of the M.G., having just emerged from under it.*

MARK: Try it, will you, sweetheart?

> *The wheels start to twist as* JOANNA *tests the steering.*

MARK: Now the other way. Fine. Let's go.

> *The engine starts.* MARK *runs to get round and in.* JOANNA *revs and starts the car up the steep slope the path takes to get to the road.*

MARK: Plenty of revs.

> *The engine roars. The car goes from us up the slope. It stops. The engine dies.*
> *The car rolls back down the slope.* JOANNA *grins.*

JOANNA: We stalled.
MARK: You stalled.
JOANNA: You drive.
MARK: No, no ...
JOANNA: I don't want to drive.

> MARK *changes places with* JOANNA *and starts the car in businesslike fashion. It charges away up towards the slope. It revs furiously. It stops as the engine dies. It rolls back into shot and stops.* JOANNA *looks at* MARK.

JOANNA: You stalled.

> MARK *sits hunched in fury. He starts the car again.*

## 56. EXT. *THE SLOPE. DAY.*
*The car comes back into shot – the only way to get it up the slope has been in reverse.*

JOANNA: Done it!

> JOANNA *gives* MARK *a slick look and changes gear and moves off smartly. There is a terrible clang.* MARK's *expression changes.*

76

*He looks at her like it was her fault. He gets out in a rage and looks under the car.*

*The pipe has parted again.* MARK *looks round furiously.*

*There are some rags in a heap by the gate they've just come out of.* MARK *picks them up.*

MARK: There's more rust than pipe!

*He goes under the car.*

JOANNA *waits for him. He comes out.*

MARK: That'll hold for a while.

*She slides over. He gets in and starts the car.*

## 57. EXT. *ROAD. DAY.*
*The M.G. bowling along.* MARK *sniffs.*

MARK: Someone's having a bonfire.
JOANNA: I love bonfires. (*She sniffs and smiles.*) One day we're going to have a big, big garden and grow lots of bonfires.

MARK *drives on sniffing again.*

## 57a. EXT. *ROAD.*
*The M.G. eases past until we are following it, from a low angle. Sparks are coming out of the exhaust and there is a curl of dark smoke coming from under the car.*

MARK: The smell I like best is wood smoke. Hickory smoke, for instance. You ever smell hickory smoke?
JOANNA: Never.

## 57b. INT. *MOVING CAR. DAY.*
MARK: I have to take you to the States. Alternatively, I could get Cathy to send us a few cans. They really can it, you know. She could.
JOANNA: Or she could bring some on her next visit.

MARK *raises his eyebrows.*

MARK: Don't tell me I detect a welcoming note.

JOANNA (*mock American accent*): You wouldn't want her not to come and see your dear little baby, would you?
MARK: No.

*He looks at her in alarm.*

MARK: You're not?

*She nods gaily.*

MARK: And that, I suppose, was my little holiday surprise?
JOANNA: I don't suppose it's really much of a surprise.
MARK: Well, you know ...

*He gives her a big hug.*

MARK: You always have to have what you want, don't you?

*She makes a face, lips pressed together, eyes bulging. He puts his hand flat on her belly.*

MARK: Aren't we supposed to celebrate? What've we got to drink?

JOANNA *produces a bottle of mineral water. She pours some into a mug and hands it to him.*

57c. *THE ROAD. DAY.*

MARK: Here's to it.
JOANNA: It.

*Smoke billows out behind, unnoticed. Some PEOPLE in another car, coming towards them, wave and point. MARK and JOANNA wave back. The M.G. has once again edged through frame so that it is now going away from us. It is completely obscured now by a cloud of black smoke, of which MARK and JOANNA remain oblivious.*

58. EXT. *ANTIQUE YARD. DAY.*
*The Mercedes is parked in view.*

MARK *and* JOANNA *are looking at the display.*

MARK (*justifying himself*): If you design a house for people, you have to take them a house-warming present.

78

JOANNA: People with stereophonic under-floor ducted heating don't need house-warming presents.

*She stops in front of a huge stone lady with prodigious breasts and hips.*

MARK (*nods to it*): So nice to have met you both.

*He smiles at JOANNA, who grins back, a little ruefully.*

MARK (*takes her hand*): As soon as we've finished with Maurice and Co. let's go off somewhere and just be ourselves.

JOANNA: I doubt if you'll be able to spare the time.

MARK (*angrily*): You don't want us to succeed!

JOANNA (*in front of a large wrought-iron negro with a pineapple on his head*): How about this for their living-pit? No?

MARK (*hurt boy*): Why be sarcastic?

JOANNA: Sarcastic?

MARK: About the living-pit. That's what it's called. A depressed section in the middle of a room. It's called a living-pit.

JOANNA: I called it a living-pit. What's sarcastic about calling a living-pit a living-pit?

MARK: You think my work's some kind of a joke.

*They wander sourly for a moment.*

MARK (*grins suddenly*): What the hell kind of expression is 'living-pit' anyway?

JOANNA: I love you.

*He looks at her solemnly, suddenly sad. And pleased.*

MARK: I won't let it all go up in smoke, Joanna, I won't.

JOANNA: What's going up in smoke?

59. EXT. *THE ROAD. DAY.*
*The M.G. is pouring flames from underneath – but JOANNA and MARK are, for another moment, unaware of the catastrophe.*

59a. INT. *MOVING M.G. DAY.*
*JOANNA and MARK, happily sitting in the front.*

MARK: We're getting farther south all right.

JOANNA: It's certainly getting warmer.
MARK: Right.

> *A hooting behind – Boopety-boop-boop-booooooooop!*

## 59b. EXT. *THE ROAD. DAY.*

MARK *puts his foot down. The car behind comes up alongside them and the* PASSENGERS *point furiously.*

MARK: If they're going to overtake, why don't they overtake?

> *He signals them on. They point again.* JOANNA *smiles and then looks back. Flames are coming up behind the hood.*

JOANNA: Mark! Fire!
MARK: Where?
JOANNA: Here. Us. We are on fire.

> MARK *looks back and the car practically swerves off the road. They zigzag crazily to a halt.*

## 59c. EXT. *DOMAINE ST JUSTE. DAY.*

*The other car has vanished ahead. The area is deserted. No sign of water. They leap out and* MARK *attacks the flames with his jacket. But they are too strong.*

MARK: Water.
JOANNA: Where?

> *He starts to drag the luggage out of the back and chucks it into the side of the road – the tent, etcetera.*

MARK: Find some.

> JOANNA *looks around desperately. She takes the bottle of mineral water from the front and with a helpless sort of shrugging loyalty pours its contents on to the flames. They spring higher.*

JOANNA: It likes water!

> *The flames are unquenchable.*

MARK: We must have more water!

> JOANNA *looks around. The only sign of life is the entrance to a very ritzy-looking country hotel, the Domaine St Juste.*

JOANNA: It's no good.

> *She comes up and tries to help him with the blankets, etc.*

MARK: You don't have to tell me. Stand back.

JOANNA (*hoping he's going to perform some miracle*): What're you going to do?

MARK: I'm going to stand back. Think I'm crazy?

> *The flames mount higher. In the distance, sirens are heard. Some people come running out of the hotel entrance and stand watching. MADAME, the owner, is toting a bucket of water, which they fling hopelessly on to the flames.*

MADAME: I have telephoned the pumpers.

JOANNA: The Fire Brigade.

> MARK *nods and tries futilely to think of something to do.*

## 59d. EXT. *DOMAINE. DAY.*

*A spout of asbestos foam squirts from a fire hose and then stops. The flames are dead. And so is the M.G. In the middle of an appalling mess the car sits snowed up in white asbestos foam. We pan across to* JOANNA *who is soaked from head to foot and also daubed with foam.* MARK *is blackened and sad. Funeral music.*

*Cars file past along the water-drenched, foam-slicked main road in an almost mournful procession, with* GENDARMES *acting as ushers.* FIREMEN *push the wreck into the side. Rotating lights on the fire engines and the Gendarmerie vans add a note of delusive gaiety.*

MADAME *drapes a blanket round* JOANNA.

*The* INSPECTOR *of the Gendarmerie and the* CHEF DES POMPIERS *are consulting together. The* INSPECTOR *comes up to* MARK.

INSPECTOR: Passeport, s'il vous plaît, Monsieur.

> MARK *nods and feels for his passport. There is a tap on his shoulder. He turns.* JOANNA, *wrapped in a blanket, holds up his passport.*
>
> *A Rolls Royce comes by. In it, though we do not know them by name at the moment, are* FRANÇOISE *and* MAURICE DALBRET.

FRANÇOISE *is a chic, blonde Frenchwoman (though she speaks perfect seductive English), and* MAURICE *is a charming, middle-aged, supremely confident and egotistical Frenchman. The* DALBRETS *are very rich. Their car has French number plates. They pass the wreck and look at it with intrigued amusement. The Rolls Royce drives up to the front of the Domaine.*

60. INT./EXT. *THE FORD. HOTEL YARD. DAY.*
*The Ford turns in and drives up to an hotel.*
*Inside:*

CATHY: For heaven's sake park it in the shade this time, Howie, I don't want to come out after lunch to a red-hot car again.

> JOANNA *and* MARK *exchange a secret look.* HOWARD *nods and steers toward a high, palm-leaf-roofed carport. He drives in and pulls up. A sign faces them:* POUR LA DIRECTION.

HOWARD: What does 'pour la direction' (*he pronounces the words as if they were English*) mean?

JOANNA: Reserved for the management.

HOWARD: Hell, we're the customers.

RUTH: Daddy, why do you think Red China is a bitch?

CATHY: We can't stay here, Howie.

> JOANNA *and* MARK *look at each other and then don't say anything.*

HOWARD: I meant Red China is a difficult problem. It's all right, Cathy, I'm moving. I'm moving.

> *He revs up and shoots out backwards at great speed and with much crunching of gravel.*

> *We now see a row of low concrete sun-shaded carports.* HOWARD *changes gear grindingly.*

CATHY: Over there, Howie, is perfect.

HOWARD: I saw them.

> *He accelerates at great speed again and hurtles under the low lintel. There is an appalling crash. The concrete lintel was quite high enough for a normal car, but the Ford has a roof rack stacked high*

*with luggage and this has hit the concrete beam with great force. The luggage has been dragged backwards and knocked sideways and generally sent flying.*

*There is a long silence.*

RUTH: Daddy.

*Another long silence.*

HOWARD: Yes, Ruthie.

RUTH: Daddy, did you do that on purpose?

*Another silence.*

HOWARD (*very quickly indeed*): No, Ruthie, I didn't. I did not. No. No, I didn't. No.

*Another case falls from the roof and dangles on its elastic strap, bobbing up and down silently outside the window.*

*A fly buzzes against the windscreen, and with manic zest* HOWARD *gets the aerosol fly-killer and squirts it to death or tries to.*


## 61. INT. *BATHROOM. BEDROOM. DOMAINE ST JUSTE. DAY.*

JOANNA *squirts the hand-shower all over* MARK *who is in the bath, luxuriating, though still black with smoke and soot from the M.G. fire.*

MARK: What the hell are you …

JOANNA: Do you love me?

MARK: Now she asks! Don't you …

JOANNA: Do you?

MARK: Confessions extracted under torture don't count, don't you know that? (*Yells*) YES! You'll get us turned out of here. (*Pause*) That's not such a bad idea! It's going to ruin us anyway.

*He starts to get out of the bath.*

JOANNA *is now in the bedroom and goes to the window.*

JOANNA: This is heaven. I could eat a horse.

*She flings open the shutters.*

83

MARK *is studying the price list on the back of the door. He is wrapped in a towel.*

MARK: You may have to. I hate to tell you this, but we've just gone on a diet.

JOANNA: We didn't have any lunch!

MARK: Baby, I'm not kidding, we can't afford to eat here.

JOANNA: Oh!

MARK: No.

JOANNA *looks through the mess of stuff. She holds up a bag of squashed tomatoes – very squashed.*

JOANNA: Supper!

*She starts undressing and goes into the bathroom.*

MARK (*calls*): We shall just have to practise self-restraint.

## 62. INT. *THE BATHROOM. DAY.*
JOANNA *is sitting in the bath.* MARK *comes in.*

JOANNA (*reciting as in a trance*): I am not hungry. You are not hungry. We are not hungry.

JOANNA *comes out of her trance and looks at him.*

JOANNA: I'm hungry. *You* are not hungry.

MARK: A woman in an advanced state of pregnancy should be very careful about over-eating.

JOANNA: Advanced! I have eight months to go. There must be a food shop in the village.

MARK: And I'm too worried about you to dream of eating anything. I'm just going to slip down to the chemist to get you some – what do you think?

JOANNA. Hamburgers.

MARK: Tablets. That's it. Tablets.

*He takes a large sack from the pile of stuff.*

JOANNA: Hamburger tablets. Large hamburger tablets. And don't let them see you bringing them in.

## 63. EXT. *ROAD FROM VILLAGE. DAY.*

MARK *is trekking along carrying a paper sack of provisions, looking glum and slouchy. It is rather overcast, spitting rain gently. The white Mercedes sweeps into view and blots out the trekking figure.*

## 64. INT. *MERCEDES. DAY.*

*The roof is up against the rain. The gilt figure is in the back with* JOANNA'S *overnight bag.*

MARK: What about food?

JOANNA: What about food?

MARK: We have to eat. Let's go to the Domaine St Juste. Why not?

JOANNA: I'm not dressed.

MARK: Baby, the last time we went there I was dressed in soot and you were wearing a blanket.

JOANNA: I can change, if you want me to.

MARK: Change. I want you to.

> *He smiles across at her. She reaches in the back and opens her travelling bag. She pulls out a brilliant cocktail dress of red silk and starts to wriggle out of her clothes.*

## 65. EXT. *THE ROAD. DAY.*

*A Fiat overtakes them. The* DRIVER *goggles at our Mercedes.*

## 66. EXT. *THE MERCEDES. DAY.*

*Through the windscreen (as from the last* DRIVER'S *p.o.v.) we see* JOANNA *with her dress entirely over her head and* MARK *driving quite unconcernedly.*

## 67. EXT. *THE ROAD. DAY.*

*The Fiat* DRIVER *looks over his shoulder, misses a corner, and drives deep into a field of high wheat in which his car is completely drowned.*

## 68. INT. *MERCEDES. DAY.*

JOANNA *finishing wriggling into the red dress.*

MARK: Are you almost there? Because we're almost there.

JOANNA: Circle around a little, will you?

MARK: We'll have to get a bigger car.

JOANNA (*wriggling*): Or a bigger dress. Phew!

MARK: You look sensational. Here we are.

JOANNA: Mark, hold it, please. I'm not done up.

    *They turn into the entrance of the Domaine St Juste.*

## 69. EXT. *DOMAINE ST JUSTE. DAY.*
*The Mercedes drives up in front of the hotel.* JOANNA *looks out, very elegant and assured. The* DOORMAN *comes out and goes towards the car.*

## 70. INT./EXT. *THE MERCEDES. DAY.*
JOANNA *turns and smiles at the oncoming* DOORMAN.

JOANNA (*through her teeth*): I'm still not done up.

    *She turns her back to* MARK, *who zips up the back of her dress.*

DOORMAN: Bonsoir, Madame.

JOANNA (*smiles politely*): Bonsoir!

    MARK's P.O.V. *He fishes desperately and finally makes the vital junction.* JOANNA *makes time by handing out various things for the* DOORMAN *to take.*

    JOANNA *finally opens the door and steps out of the car.* MARK *gets out too.*

DOORMAN: Bonsoir …

## 71. INT. *LOBBY. DOMAINE ST JUSTE. DAY.*
MADAME: … Monsieur.

    MARK *walks across the lobby, looking shabby but as casual as he can. He bulges suspiciously, but tries to look inconspicuous. He gives* MADAME *a sickly smile.*

MARK: Bonsoir, Madame.

    *He goes towards the stairs.*

MADAME: Bon appétit!

    *He starts guiltily and smiles seedily. But he looks round to see that she is speaking to some other* GUESTS. *He continues up the stairs.*

*He reaches the first landing when* FRANÇOISE *and* MAURICE *come down.* MARK *steps back politely to allow them passage. They nod, without smiling, and go past.* MARK *slightly misses his footing and grabs at the balustrade. A tomato falls out of his sleeve and rolls, in full view.*

MARK *starts after it and begins to spill other food.* FRANÇOISE *retrieves the tomato and hands it back to* MARK. MARK *smiles awfully and trudges on up.*

## 72. INT. *THE ROOM. DAY.*
JOANNA *opens the door.* MARK *comes in.*

MARK: Phew!

> *He shakes himself. Good food literally falls from him. The last thing he produces is a bottle of cheap wine. He goes into the bathroom and returns with the two toothglasses. He pulls the cork out of the wine bottle.*

## 73. INT. *RESTAURANT OF DOMAINE ST JUSTE. NIGHT.*
*Wine being poured for* JOANNA *in her red, elegant dress.* MARK *and* JOANNA *sip their wine. They can't think of anything to say now.* JOANNA *toys with her food.*

JOANNA: What sort of people just sit in restaurants and don't even try to talk to each other?

MARK (*looks up and smiles wryly*): Married people.

> *They smile with real amusement and touch glasses to each other.*

## 74. *CORRIDOR. NIGHT.*
*A severe* CHAMBERMAID *comes out of the next room, having done the bed, turns out the light and comes to* MARK *and* JOANNA'S *door. She knocks briefly and opens the door.*

## 75. INT. *THE ROOM. NIGHT.*
CHAMBERMAID'S P.O.V. JOANNA *lying with the coverlet right up to her chin, apparently in a fitful doze.* MARK *is reading a book with an air*

*of solemn anxiety.* MARK *raises his finger to his lips. The* CHAMBER-MAID *nods and goes out, contrite.*

MARK *continues chewing food. He pulls back the coverlet and reveals the entire picnic still laid out: ham, sardines, fruit, etc.*

MARK: You're the only woman I know who's prepared to share her bed with a sardine.

JOANNA *kisses him.*

JOANNA: I don't care what kind of a sardine you are, I like you. Are you going to hate me when I'm bow-fronted?

MARK: Undoubtedly.

JOANNA: Will you be unfaithful to me?

MARK: Blatantly.

JOANNA: No.

MARK: You promised I could!

JOANNA: Yes, but you promised you wouldn't. (*Explains*) When we got married.

## 76. INT. *BEDROOM. DOMAINE ST JUSTE. NIGHT.*

MARK *is working at a spread-out pile of plans and blueprints. The red dress comes into shot and* JOANNA *turns her back to him.*

JOANNA: Would you mind undoing what you did?

*He reaches up, almost without looking, and unzips her dress, unhooks her bra.*

JOANNA: Thanks.

MARK: Welcome.

*He goes on working as she moves out of shot and continues undressing.*

JOANNA: Are you coming to bed at all?

MARK: Tired?

JOANNA (*innocently*): No.

MARK: I won't be long.

JOANNA: Shall I call your secretary and make an appointment?

MARK (*between irritation and amusement, looks up*): When did you start being as snide as this?

88

JOANNA: Right after we got married. Didn't I?

MARK: Did we get married?

JOANNA: Oh yes. Don't you remember? When sex stopped being fun.

MARK: And started being official. I remember.

*He gets up and goes and embraces her.*

## 77. INT. *THE ROOM. NIGHT.*

*The picnic is finished. The camping equipment is piled against the wardrobe. The whining of a mosquito.*

JOANNA: You know, I think that lovely little lake breeds lovely little mosquitoes.

MARK: I'll shut the window.

JOANNA: We may suffocate.

*The whining increases. He gets into bed with her.*
*She draws the sheet right over their heads.*

MARK: That's great ...

JOANNA: And just –

MARK: Except –

*We move down to the end of the bed. Their feet are now bared.*

JOANNA: They've taken our last penny. Now they're going to take our last drop of blood as well.

MARK: We'll just have to pretend they don't exist.

JOANNA: Right. Good night.

MARK: Good night.

*They settle for sleep.*

JOANNA: Mark.

MARK: Mmmm?

JOANNA: They exist.

MARK: No, they don't.

*He leaps up.*

MARK: Yes, they do.

JOANNA: I've had an idea.

## 78. INT. *THE ROOM. DAY.*

*It is the following morning. Start on the window and move across to the bed. The igloo tent has been inflated to make a mosquito-proof vault over the bed.* JOANNA *reaches round and takes the plug out of the tent. It subsides and she pushes it off on to the floor.*

MARK: Sleep well?

JOANNA: Very well. I had the most dreamy dream.

MARK: Well, tell me the worst.

JOANNA: I dreamt you built us the most beautiful Wallace-designed house –

MARK: Uh-huh!

JOANNA: And I built us the most beautiful little Wallace-designed triplets. Wasn't that lovely?

> *She turns her blissful face to* MARK *who looks at her with calculated lack of excitement.*

MARK: All we need right now is a population explosion.

> *There is a knock at the door.*

MARK: Who is it?

> *The door opens and the* CHAMBERMAID *comes in with a beautiful breakfast tray with coffee, rolls, croissants, honey, cake, flowers, morning paper, etc.*

CHAMBERMAID: Oh, you did not need the mosquito net?

> MARK *and* JOANNA *look up. A white gauze cocoon is tied up to a hook in the ceiling.* JOANNA *and* MARK *look at each other. A mosquito net!*

JOANNA: No. We managed without.

> *The* CHAMBERMAID *shrugs and puts the tray down near them. They shake their heads.*

CHAMBERMAID (*astonished*): No breakfast?

> *They shake their heads.* JOANNA *sees a cross round the* CHAMBERMAID's *neck.*

JOANNA (*explains*): Religious reasons, Madame.

*The* CHAMBERMAID *nods and takes the breakfast away. She shuts the door.* JOANNA *and* MARK *look hungrily at each other.*

MARK: Let's get out of here. This self-denial is killing me.

## 79. INT. *LOBBY. DOMAINE ST JUSTE. DAY.*

JOANNA *and* MARK *come downstairs with all their camping equipment.* MADAME *is at the cash desk as* MARK *approaches. She has the bill ready.*

MADAME: I am so sorry you were not able to sample our restaurant last night.

MARK: Yes, so are we. Religious reasons.

*He makes polite gestures.*

MADAME: Particularly when we have to charge you an all-inclusive price, as you see –

MARK (*stunned, studies the bill*): I beg your pardon?

MADAME: High season – our price includes dinner and breakfast always.

MARK *gulps and takes out his wallet, pays the bill.*

MADAME: Thank you. I think the Inspector is waiting for you outside, Monsieur.

MARK: Inspector?

MADAME: Concerning the expenses for the pumpers and such like.

MARK *nods.*

MAURICE *and* FRANÇOISE, *unsmiling as ever, come up behind him and* MAURICE *signals for his bill.* MAURICE *and* FRANÇOISE *look bleakly at each other.*

MADAME: We will see you again, I hope.

*They smile grimly and go towards the door.*

MARK (*to* JOANNA): What's the French for 'Inspector, that is a damn lie and I am not going to pay a penny'?

JOANNA: Oui, Monsieur.

## 80. EXT. *DOMAINE ST JUSTE. DAY.*

MARK *and* JOANNA *have met the* INSPECTOR *by the Rolls Royce and walk slowly down the gravel drive with him.*

MARK: Oui, Monsieur.

INSPECTOR: Trente mille francs.

MARK: Oui, Monsieur.

INSPECTOR: Et cinq mille plus deux mille cinq cents plus deux mille cinq cents plus deux mille cinq cents. C'est tout.

MARK: C'est tout?

INSPECTOR: C'est tout.

> MARK *looks puzzled. The* INSPECTOR *points. The M.G. en son goo. The mess at the side of the road.* MARK *shrugs.* JOANNA *looks helplessly at him from the roadside.*

INSPECTOR: Et mille francs taxe.

MARK (*the last straw*): Taxe!?

INSPECTOR: Taxe.

MARK: Taxe on what?

> JOANNA *goes and joins them.*

JOANNA: Quel taxe, Monsieur l'Inspecteur?

INSPECTOR: Taxe sur quarante-deux mille cinq cents francs, Madame.

MARK: Mille francs?

INSPECTOR: Mille francs.

JOANNA: Pourquoi mille francs sur quarante-deux mille cinq cents?

INSPECTOR: Taxe.

JOANNA: Mais pourquoi mille francs?

INSPECTOR: Mille francs de taxe, Madame.

MARK: This is literally highway robbery! It's literally highway robbery!

JOANNA (*out of gritted teeth, still smiling*): Don't lose your temper.

MARK: I AM NOT LOSING MY TEMPER.

> MARK *empties his wallet into the* INSPECTOR'S *hands.*

INSPECTOR: Et dix mille francs pour en disposer.

*He gestures to the wreck.*

JOANNA: For disposing of the wreck.
MARK: We'll dispose of it. Nous la disposerons.
INSPECTOR: Mais, où …
JOANNA: Where will we?
MARK: Quelque place ou autre. Come on, Jo.

## 81. EXT. *HILL. THE ROAD. DAY.*
MARK *and* JOANNA *are pushing the M.G. It is on its rims, a terrible, toasted ruin. It begins to run freely down the hill.*

JOANNA *and* MARK *look back at the Domaine and when they turn back to the car it is going too quickly for them. It careers down the hill and fails to make the corner at the bottom. It goes between two stone gate posts, dislodging them like children's bricks. The stone balls on top of the posts crash into the gateway. The car storms on and goes into a large Dutch barn whose towering thatch roof is supported on a central column. The car hits the column and the entire roof comes down over the car like a lid.*

JOANNA *looks appalled.*

MARK: We disposed of it.

> *The* FARMER *now appears shaking with rage.* MARK *ruefully discloses his empty wallet. Meanwhile the Rolls Royce has come into shot.* MAURICE *and* FRANÇOISE *are rocking with laughter. The* FARMER *is raving about Police and Scandale and Dommages and Poursuites Judiciaires. We close on his face which slowly clears from anger to suspicion to reluctance to amiability to good humour.*

> *Ease back to disclose* MAURICE *feeding notes into the* FARMER'S *honest peasant hand.* FRANÇOISE *is leaning helplessly against the pump in the farmyard in agonized hysterics of laughter.*

## 82. INT./EXT. *THE ROLLS. THE ROAD. DAY.*
MARK *and* JOANNA, *dazed but delighted, are sitting in the back of the car.*

MARK (*whispers*): This is the life.

FRANÇOISE *looks quite recovered from the giggles.*

MAURICE (*ending a story*): He let me down, I must tell you, disgracefully. So I am looking for an architect.

JOANNA *looks at* MARK. MARK *shakes his head: don't tell him.*

JOANNA: My husband is an architect.

FRANÇOISE *goes into fits of giggles. They look at her. She shakes her head, recovering herself.*

FRANÇOISE: You put up buildings as well as knocking them down?

MARK: Corporation bus –

JOANNA (*quickly*): He never has a spare moment.

MAURICE: What about now?

JOANNA: He has a spare moment.

MAURICE: Good, good. Good. We must talk. I must tell you I am really in a corner.

MARK *makes a face: oh well, if you insist.*

*The Rolls cuts shamelessly on an American station wagon which has to brake sharply.*

MAURICE: Espèce de chewing gum!

83. EXT. *THE FORD. THE ROAD. DAY.*
*The Rolls cuts right across in front of* HOWARD, *who brakes sharply.*

84. INT. *THE FORD. DAY.*
HOWARD: Communist!

*They have all fallen forward with the speed of the braking and various pieces of luggage have fallen on* JOANNA *and* MARK *who are again in the back seats.*

*They extricate themselves as the car moves forward again.*

HOWARD (*sees road sign*): Chantilly. Now that's in the guide book … ?

MARK: It could just be.

JOANNA: Oh do let's stop!

CATHY: I don't want Ruthie to be late for her lunch today.
HOWARD: It's off the main road.
MARK: Listen, Howard, before we get to Greece, maybe I should warn you, the Acropolis is off the main road.
HOWARD: O.K. O.K., this is a democratic trip.

## 85. EXT. *CHANTILLY. DAY.*
*The Ford drives in. They all get out.* HOWARD *looks meaningly at his watch.*

## 86. SPEEDED-UP SEQUENCE. *CHANTILLY. DAY.*
*The sequence includes the tour of the château, with everybody taking souvenir photographs of everybody else with everybody else. The tour resumes at breakneck speed up and down the steps with the help of a* GUIDE *whose explanatory speech is also speeded up. Then they are out again and into the car and driving away.*

## 87. INT. *THE FORD. DAY.*
HOWARD: It really is great to dawdle through an old place like that. Joanna, I have to thank you.
RUTH: I thought you didn't like Joanna, Daddy.
HOWARD: Of course I like Joanna.
RUTH: Then why did Mommy say she was a suburban English nobody?

*There is a long silence.*

HOWARD: I think it may be very important for the future of our quadripartite relationship to get that particular remark into very clear context.
MARK: It might be best for the future of our quadripartite relationship if we accepted here and now (*fiercely*) that it has no future whatsoever.

MARK *opens the door of the car.*

## 88. EXT. *SMALL TOWN. DAY.*
MARK *is trying to extract their suitcase from the very careful arrangement*

*on the roof. He starts unlooping the elastic straps, chucking other cases to the ground, and so on.*

HOWARD: Mark, please don't be too hasty –

MARK: We're through, Howard, we're through –

HOWARD: Those things took a lot of arranging. Now you listen to me – try and imagine how Joanna feels –

MARK: I can see how Joanna feels.

HOWARD: She's going to feel that the whole trip's been loused up because of her.

MARK: You are the most complacent sonofagun –

HOWARD: Abuse me if you want to –

MARK: I want to –

HOWARD: You're going to dominate that girl out of existence.

MARK: I'm going to smash your face in, Howard, now –

HOWARD: That's not a very adult attitude, if I may say so. Mark, please, that's the phonograph. Marcus, please.

> MARK *is still handling the luggage very roughly, extracting their belongings.*

MARK: Come on, Joanna. Darling, come on, sweetheart.

> *He calls her through the car window.*
>
> MARK *opens the car door.* JOANNA *gets out.*

HOWARD: You haven't thought of asking Joanna if she wants to abandon the expedition at this point, now have you?

MARK (*to* JOANNA): Come on, baby.

HOWARD: That, if I may say so, is a very revealing usage. Calling her 'baby' at this point shows that you are prepared to do her thinking and her deciding for her – I warn you solemnly, Marcus, you're denying Joanna the right to be her own paradoxical self.

MARK: Howard, you are the largest untapped pocket of natural gas known to man.

## 89. EXT. *SMALL TOWN. DAY.*

*A large petrol-tanker passes through and out of frame. The street is visible from where* MARK *and* JOANNA *have been in the last scene. But as the tanker pulls clear, we see the pair of them ambling along, the*

96

*carefree hitch-hiking students again. They come to a shop which is being redecorated. A* SIGN-WRITER *is at work on the window, carefully painting in the owner's name and telephone number.* MARK *and* JOANNA *stop to look.*

## 90. INT. *THE SHOP. DAY.*
*Through the window which the* SIGN-WRITER *continues to work on,* MARK *and* JOANNA *are looking in at the* OWNER *and his* WIFE *who are having, very obviously, one hell of a row. Since the* P.O.V. *is from the outside, we cannot hear a word, but their dumb show is even more eloquent than their words. They slam, they yell, they shrug, they threaten.*

## 91. EXT. *THE STREET. DAY.*
MARK *and* JOANNA *hugging each other with amusement and barely able to contain themselves.*

MARK: And they haven't even opened yet.
JOANNA: What do you think it's about?
MARK: Who knows?
JOANNA: What do people have rows about?
MARK: Money. Sex. Sex. Money. He wants. She doesn't want.
JOANNA: She wants. He doesn't want.
MARK (*peers in*): He thinks that counter is all in the wrong place.
JOANNA: The counter. The display case. It's really funny!
MARK: That's marriage for you.
JOANNA: That's marriage for them.
MARK: That's marriage. Full stop.

## 92. INT. *THE SHOP. DAY.*
MARK *and* JOANNA's p.o.v. *The row gets even fiercer. But now* MARK's *and* JOANNA's *voices are heard while we see the shop owners arguing.*

MARK: I'm allowed not to like Howard and Cathy. They're my friends. You never intended to enjoy the trip. You were jealous of Cathy before we ever set out.
JOANNA: It's not my idea of bliss to be cooped in a car with three

Maxwell Manchesters.

MARK: You promised me that once we were married, you'd always be happy, no matter what.

JOANNA: I know.

MARK: Well then, why can't you be happy no matter what?

JOANNA: Because I can't.

*A pause.*

MARK: Then you've broken your promise.

*A pause.*

JOANNA: I am happy usually.

*A pause.*

JOANNA (*makes a face: so?*): I love you, if that's any good.

MARK (*grudgingly*): That's not the issue.

JOANNA: If it isn't, it should be. The issue!

MARK: You're right.

JOANNA: I'm right?

MARK: You're right. Let's find an hotel.

JOANNA: It's three o'clock in the afternoon. What do we want an hotel for?

*He looks at her.*

JOANNA: Let's find an hotel.

*She gets up and takes his arm. He kisses her. They go away from us.*

MARK: To hell with the Maxwell Manchesters. Mr, Mrs and Miss. From now on, we travel alone together or not at all.

*A Triumph Herald comes along the village street and cuts us off from them.*

## 93. EXT. *VILLAGE STREET. DAY.*

*The Herald is coming down to the end of the village.* MARK *is driving it. He is alone in the car. It is four years later. On the back of the car is a sticker: 'Running In – Please Pass'.*

## 93a. *THE ROAD. HERALD. DAY.*

MARK (V.O.): My darling Joanna, So far all goes well. The car's nearly run in and my patience is nearly run out. I miss you like mad. I drove nearly all night last night – couldn't face one of our hotels without you with me. I finally slept in the car quite near where we buried the poor old burnt-out M.G.

93b. EXT. *ROAD. DAY.*
*As this 'letter' is being read over, there is a sudden erk-erk and a Saab convertible overtakes the Herald. A single blonde* GIRL *is in it, her hair blowing in the wind, her face full-lipped, blue-eyed, confident, a little coarse. She is about 32.*

*She turns and looks at* MARK *and then accelerates on down the road.*

MARK (v.o.): I wish to hell I hadn't had to make the trip, but I suppose what with the house, not to mention The Terror, otherwise Caroline, it's just as well I've got some work. At least this pays better than corporation bus shelters.

> *He has driven on round a bend in the road. The Saab is going very slowly up a mild gradient and he repasses it with a smile at the* GIRL *who is driving it.*

MARK (v.o.): And it's a lot more interesting, too, let's face it. I think about you all the time.

> *The Saab now recovers its zing and comes up and overtakes again.* MARK *knows a signal when it's flashed right in his face. The two cars now begin to race each other. The daring of the race increases as the sexual attraction between the two drivers becomes more flagrant.* MARK *tackles back – then she roars past – the pace gets more furious and the chances taken more outrageous.*

94. EXT. *TUNNEL. ROAD. DAY.*
*Top shot: The Saab goes into the tunnel first, closely followed by the Herald. We pan along the top of the ridge through which the tunnel goes. The Herald comes out first, followed by the Saab.*

MARK (v.o.): It's been a pretty uneventful drive so far. It's a long dull road when you're on your own. All I care about is getting down there, doing whatever has to be done and getting the hell back. When I'm not being woken at three in the morning I feel very paternal and I miss you both (that sounds funny still somehow) more than I can say. Life's very flat.

*During the last part of this we hold on the Saab and the very handsome* GIRL *in it. Her name is actually* SIMONE. *She looks very good.*

## 95. EXT. *VILLAGE. DAY.*

*A carnival in progress. These hangovers from fertility festivals take place all over the South of France. Everyone is in fancy dress, with masks, and the village brass band plays ponderously festal music while the people dance. The* REVELLERS *carry long poles with 'horses' tails' of coloured paper at the end and with these the males tap any passing female, the females any passing male. The whole street is filled with them, the procession threads through the streets which are bright with lights. It continues and we, swept along with the music, move on with it as it goes round a corner.*

MARK (V.O.): I shall probably drive on overnight tonight and get down to the site in the morning. Two or three sessions with the far-famed clients should be more than enough.

*The procession passes a small hotel. There are two cars parked outside: the Saab and the Herald.*

MARK (V.O.): It's typical of me that as soon as I get away, all I want to do is get back to you again.

*We pan up to a bedroom window in the hotel.*

## 96. INT. *THE HOTEL ROOM. NIGHT.*

SIMONE *shakes her head and lies, catlike, under the sheet on the big bed. She watches as* MARK (*not visible to us*) *comes closer to her. We move in with him.* MARK'S *hand now comes and takes the sheet and lifts it right along and off her.*

*He puts the sheet over the end of the bed in which her bare legs are now visible. He smiles. She smiles.*

*The light goes out.*

MARK (V.O.): I won't write any more at the moment, because I really do want to get on. As soon as I have a chance, I'll drop you another line. Love, love, love – Mark.

## 97. EXT. *FORK IN ROAD. DAY.*
*The Saab and the Herald come along. The Saab is leading. Both are travelling at speed. The Saab forks off towards Marseille. The Herald sheers away from it along the other fork. The two cars move farther and farther apart.*

MARK (V.O.): P.S. The next time we come away, we shall have our own little Ruthiebelle with us.

## 98. EXT. *TUNNEL. DAY.*
*The Herald goes in with* MARK *alone driving – and the theme of* SIMONE *fading slowly in our ears.*

## 99. EXT. *THE TUNNEL (FAR END). DAY.*
*The Herald comes out with* MARK, JOANNA *and* CAROLINE *in it. The car is dented in one wing and a fender is slightly twisted at one end. It's been used.*

## 99a. INT. HERALD. *DAY.*
CAROLINE *is two and a half. She doesn't talk a great deal, but she is a pretty, alert child, not too angelic, but with none of* RUTH's *assertive ghastliness. She is eating an ice-cream out of a tub and spilling a good deal of it down her front.*

CAROLINE: I don't want any more.

> JOANNA *takes the tub from her and scrubs unsuccessfully at the mess on her sweater.*

JOANNA: Want to finish it?

> MARK *shakes his head. He drives on.*

## 100. EXT. *THE ROAD. DAY.*
MARK *and* JOANNA *on their first trip. They are hiking, rather tired, along the road, eating out of a single tub of ice-cream – one bite for him,*

one bite for her. He feeds her a huge lump to finish with. She shakes her head, but he crams it all in. She stops and kisses him. There is a rumble of thunder.

101. EXT. *THE ROAD. DAY.*
*Specks of rain falling on the windscreen of the Herald.*

*The car stops.*

*They start to put up the top.*

102. EXT. *THE ROAD. DAY.*
*Rain falling as* JOANNA *and* MARK *hike steadily onwards.*

*Cars ignore them.*

103. INT. *HOTEL BEDROOM. DAY. RAIN.*
*A cot being manoeuvred into the room by a rather surly* CHAMBERMAID. *The hotel is fairly simple and the room small.* CAROLINE *is playing on the floor while* JOANNA *tries to get her into her pyjamas.*

JOANNA: Boiled egg for supper, Caro?

    MARK *sits on the bed and opens his briefcase.* CAROLINE *nods.*

JOANNA: Un œuf à la coq – trois minutes et demie – et du lait, s'il vous plaît. Et du pain.
CHAMBERMAID: Bien.

    MARK *has some plans out now and is considering them – an impression of small villas in an idyllic setting is among them.*

JOANNA (*not seeing what he's doing*): Make sure Caro doesn't fall out of the window or eat any of the chairs or anything, darling, can you, while I wash out a few things for the morning?
MARK: O.K.

    *She takes a pile of dirty washing for* CAROLINE *and goes into the bathroom.*

104. EXT. *THE ROAD. DAY. RAIN.*
JOANNA *and* MARK *are drenched to the skin. We start on* JOANNA

*wringing water out of the khaki knitted cap of* MARK's *which she is wearing to keep the rain off.* MARK *walks on ahead.*

*Thunder and lightning.* MARK *turns.* JOANNA *has disappeared.* MARK *blinks. The road is straight and without sign of habitation at this point. He frowns and looks in the ditch. There is a long section of concrete drainage tubing, about a yard in diameter. He goes down suspiciously and peers into it.*

## 105. INT. *THE TUBING. DAY. RAIN.*
*Sure enough* JOANNA *is inside.*

JOANNA: Enough, I say, enough!
MARK: Mind if I join you?
JOANNA: Enter, Signor!

> *He crawls in out of the rain. He crawls towards her and she towards him. They meet and make themselves comfortable.*

MARK: First time I've stayed anywhere under the beaten track.

> *He takes her in his arms and she closes her eyes.*

## 106. INT. *HOTEL BEDROOM. DAY. RAIN.*
JOANNA *can be seen in the bathroom hanging wet clothes over rails. She comes to the door with something wet still in her hand.*

JOANNA: Hasn't it come yet?

> MARK *looks up guiltily from the bed.*

MARK: What?
JOANNA: Caro's supper.
MARK: No.
JOANNA: Couldn't you go and see what's happened to it?
MARK: By all means.

> JOANNA *looks across at* CAROLINE. *She has pulled all the tissues out of a box of Kleenex and is throwing them out of the window.*

JOANNA: I thought you were watching Caroline.
MARK: I'm sorry. I have to see His Majesty The Client tomorrow morning and –

JOANNA: I'll go.
MARK: I'll go.
JOANNA: Don't bother –
MARK: Joanna, I'll go.

> *He pushes her out of the way and goes angrily to the door. Hold on* JOANNA's *face. She goes and starts putting the Kleenex back in the box. We hear* MARK's *voice, muffled, from below – and then another voice. They become increasingly angry.*

## 107. INT. *HOTEL LANDING. DAY. RAIN.*

MARK (*calling downwards*): Half an hour. Une demi-heure.
MANAGER (O.S.): C'est pas possible, Monsieur. Le chef n'est pas arrivé.
MARK: Quel chef? Pour un œuf?

> *The* MANAGER *climbs up into shot.*

MANAGER: I must ask you, Monsieur –
MARK: I must ask you, Monsieur –
MANAGER: You are disturbing the other guests –
MARK: I want that egg here within five minutes, or we're leaving.

## 108. INT. *THE ROOM. DAY. RAIN.*

MARK *bursts in.*

MARK: We're leaving.
JOANNA: Leaving?
MARK: Leaving.

> *He starts bundling all their things together.*

JOANNA: Caroline's in her pyjamas.
MARK: Then she can leave in her pyjamas. They don't want us here, we're not staying here. I'm sorry. I'm not going to be insulted by a fifth-rate doss-house and that's it.
JOANNA: I ask you for a boiled egg. You come back with an eviction order. I don't …
MARK: I've told you. We're leaving. Now let's go. Let's GO!

109. INT. *THE HERALD. NIGHT. RAIN.*
JOANNA *is sitting with* CAROLINE *still in pyjamas on her knee.* MARK *is driving. The luggage is all crammed higgledy piggledy in the back.* JOANNA *is wringing out wet clothes through the open window. Between* MARK *and* JOANNA *an atmosphere of sullen hostility.*

CAROLINE: Again, Mummy.

    JOANNA *heaves a deep sigh.*

JOANNA:    The bumble-bee, the bumble-bee,
            He flew to the top of the tulip tree,
            He flew to the top,
            But he couldn't stop,
            For he had to get home to early tea.

            The bumble-bee, the bumble-bee,
            He flew away from the tulip tree,
            But he made a mistake,
            And flew into the lakc,
            And he never got home to early tea.

110. INT. *THE TUBING. EVENING.*
MARK *and* JOANNA *asleep.*

111. INT. *CHEAP HOTEL BEDROOM. NIGHT.*
CAROLINE *asleep in a tatty cot.*

JOANNA *flings herself on the bed.*

JOANNA: Pooped!

    MARK *looks at her.*

MARK (*loudly*): Oh it's all my fault, I know.
JOANNA: I have been telling Caroline bed-time stories for one hour. It'd be nice if you could avoid fortissimo for a little while.
MARK: I quit that hotel because they didn't bring you what you wanted. I didn't want a boiled egg.
JOANNA: And Caroline, of course, is nothing to do with you.
MARK: You were the one who wanted a child.

JOANNA: Why don't you wake her up and tell her?
MARK: I don't want to tell her. I'm telling you. I love Caroline –
JOANNA (*loudly*): You don't know what love is.

> CAROLINE *starts to cry out and move.*

JOANNA (*whispers*): You don't know what love is.
MARK: That's tough on me.
JOANNA: All you can do is take the salute at an endless march-past of yourself.

> MARK *is about to get angrier, but he laughs at this image. He takes her and kisses her. She doesn't yield to him.*

MARK (*softly – ignoring her indifference*): I have an appetite. Do you?
JOANNA (*looking into his eyes*): It wouldn't matter who I was, would it?

> MARK *freezes over. He gets up and goes agitatedly to the window.*

MARK: I'm willing to call it a day. Shall we call it a day?
JOANNA: You've never wanted to call it anything else.
MARK: You're damned right there.

> JOANNA *turns and flings herself face down on the bed, without a sound.*

MARK: Joanna.

> CAROLINE *cries out.* JOANNA *immediately gets up and goes to her. There are no tears on* JOANNA's *face, but her muscles are so rigid they look tuned to a very high note indeed. She tucks in* CAROLINE *and quietens her.*

MARK: We can't even have a fight in peace.
JOANNA: Oh leave me.

> *He turns and slams his fist into the wardrobe door with a terrific crash. There is a yell from* CAROLINE.

JOANNA: You selfish ...
MARK: Oh ...

> *He goes out of the room and slams the door.*

## 112. INT. *THE BEDROOM. NIGHT.*

*The light is out. It is two hours later. The lights of cars cross the ceiling.*
JOANNA *and* MARK *lie in each other's arms in the bed. Some of the bedclothes have slipped on to the floor.* JOANNA's *nightie is among them.*
MARK *is asleep, but* JOANNA's *eyes are open.*

## 113. INT./EXT. *THE TUBE. DAY.*

*It is morning.* JOANNA *and* MARK *wake inside the tube where they have made themselves very comfortable. The tube is rocking slightly. They look at each other puzzled. They start crawling down the tube towards the daylight at the end.*

## 114. EXT. *THE ROAD. DAY.*

MARK's *and* JOANNA's *p.o.v. Cars coming up towards them and then pulling out to overtake.*

## 114a. C.U. *MARK AND JOANNA.*

*They look at each other in horror and then in delight.*

## 115. EXT. *THE ROAD. DAY.*

*A large truck with the tubing on its back climbs slowly over the brow of a hill.*

## 115a. C.U. *MARK AND JOANNA.*

*They look out of the front end of the tube (over the driving cab). They grin and hug each other.*

## 116. EXT. *THE MEDITERRANEAN. DAY.*

*The sea is there, far away but unmistakable. The coastline spread out ahead.*

## 117. EXT. *BUILDING SITE. DAY.*

*The truck with the tube on top has pulled up.* MARK *and* JOANNA *climb out and drop to the ground.*

*They walk slowly away, still bent to the shape of the tube, and slowly and painfully straighten up. They smile and take each other's hand and start skipping down the road towards the sea.*

MARK: They call it the Mediterranean, my lady!

JOANNA: Come on! Time for a swim!

> *They hurry on, breaking into a trot. They are carrying their knapsacks. They trot away.*
>
> *Dissolve to:*

## 118. EXT. *SEASIDE. DAY.*

*They are parked,* CAROLINE *is playing with her sand-bucket.* JOANNA *and* MARK *look at each other. She makes a sort of helpless face.*

MARK: I don't understand sex.

JOANNA: Don't worry. It doesn't show.

MARK: Seriously. Why is it we enjoy it more and it means less?

JOANNA: Because it's not personal any more.

MARK (*appalled*): Not personal?

JOANNA (*bluntly*): That's right.

## 119. EXT. *BEACH. SUNSET.*

JOANNA *and* MARK *trot into shot, still toting their knapsacks, some hours after descending from the lorry which carried the section of tubing. It is getting dark. They reach the fence along the promenade and lean over it, exhausted.*

MARK: Too late, they cried, too late!

> *They stare out at the sea and the lights for a long moment. Then, together, they turn and kiss passionately.* JOANNA *gives him an extra kiss afterwards.*

JOANNA: I'm so happy, I'm so happy, I'm so happy ... I wish everything could stay like this for ever.

> *He embraces her. The scene freezes for a moment, then continues.*

JOANNA: I love you. Find us a big bed.

> *She closes her eyes and opens them and smiles, as if she couldn't help herself.*

MARK: Tired?

> *She half turns and collapses, as if in a dead faint, into his arms. She opens her eyes and looks up at him from his arms.*

JOANNA: No.

MARK: Come on.

> MARK *looks across to where a low, dark embankment has a small hotel below it. He picks her up and carries her a few paces. He puts her down.*

MARK: End of romantic gesture.

JOANNA: That didn't last long.

MARK: I believe in short romances.

JOANNA: So do I. Short happy romances.

MARK: Last one in bed turns the light out.

> *They start to run towards the hotel.*

## 120. INT. *HOTEL BEDROOM. NIGHT.*

JOANNA *is in bed with the bedclothes up to her chin.* MARK *looks at her disgustedly. He reaches and pulls back the bedclothes. She is fully dressed.*

JOANNA: Oh well, it was worth a try.

> *He reaches and takes her shoes off. He starts to tickle her feet. She screams and squirms, but he continues. She falls off the bed and they roll about on the floor, laughing, kissing, laughing, serious.*

## 121. INT. *HOTEL BEDROOM. DAY.*

JOANNA: You know what I dreamt?

> *They are just waking up. The shutters are closed tight.*

MARK: What did you dream?

JOANNA: I dreamt that a train drove slap bang through the room in the middle of the night.

MARK: Sigmund Freud, what big ears you have!

JOANNA: All the better for analysing you with, my dear.

MARK: You said it.

JOANNA: It had nothing to do with sex whatever. One thing I most certainly am not is frustrated.

*She has got out of bed and goes to the window and is about to open the shutters.*

MARK: That's your story. Try and sell it to Freud.

JOANNA *flings open the shutters. Instantly there is an appalling and terrifying and thundering rattling crashing banging roaring huffing puffing. An express train roars past the window only a few feet from the sill. Carriage after carriage hurtles past while* JOANNA *and* MARK *gape. When the last carriage has gone, they gasp for air.*

JOANNA (*regaining calm*): Sexy, wasn't it?
MARK: O.K. You're not frustrated.

## 122. EXT. *SMART BEACH. DAY.*
*The Mercedes races up into the parking space and stops.*

JOANNA *and* MARK *get out. Beyond, on the beach, we can see the usual mattresses, self-conscious girls, chest-expanding, chestnut-coloured men, gaudy umbrellas, pedallos, etcetera.*

*With a sigh,* MARK *takes their swimming things out of the back of the car and they go down the concrete steps.*

## 123. EXT. *DESERTED BEACH. DAY.*
MARK *and* JOANNA *come out from behind a concrete wall (roughly matching the wall of the steps we have just seen) in their not very chic swimming things. Yet they look very good. They carry their student clothes and knapsacks.*

*They walk out on to the beach which is entirely deserted. No one in sight. They look up and shade their eyes.*

JOANNA: Hot!
MARK: Scalding already!
JOANNA: We'd better not sun too long the first day.
MARK: I don't burn. I have asbestos skin.

*He grins and claps his hands and starts to chase her furiously. She runs down to the sea and plunges in. He plunges after her.*

## 124. EXT. *DESERTED BEACH. DAY.*
*They come up out of the water and* MARK *stops and looks round the bay.*
MARK's P.O.V. *The deserted, wild hills which ring the bay.*

## 125. EXT. *THE BEACH. DAY.*
JOANNA *takes* MARK's *hand and pulls him towards the sands.*

*They come up and fling themselves down. There is a screen of bamboo half hiding them from our view. Presently her bikini and his shorts are hung over the dry bamboo. They turn over and embrace the sun.*

JOANNA: We must be very near the Garden of Eden, don't you think?

MARK: Do you know what marriage is?

JOANNA (*slightly excited*): You tell me and I'll see if we're thinking of the same thing.

MARK: Marriage is when the woman asks the man to take off his pyjamas because she wants to send them to the laundry.

*He laughs at his joke. She smiles. She stops smiling.*

MARK: Good?

JOANNA: Brilliant. I'm hungry. And thirsty.

MARK: You're never satisfied.

JOANNA: What's wrong with being hungry?

MARK: It makes you dependent on other people. It's time you realized that all human appetites are profoundly degrading, with the exception of lust.

JOANNA: What if we could just clap hands and someone'd bring us a menu.

MARK *shrugs and claps his hands.*

## 126. EXT. *SMART BEACH. DAY.*
*A* WAITER *is holding out a menu to* MARK *and* JOANNA *who lie, glistening with sun oil, on two mattresses.* MARK *has finished his order. The* WAITER *nods, makes a mark on his pad and goes.*

MARK: What if we could just clap hands and make all these people disappear?

JOANNA *claps her hands. The* WAITER *immediately turns and comes back.* JOANNA *shakes her head apologetically. The* WAITER *makes a small bow and goes away again.*

JOANNA: It's just as well. You wouldn't really like it.

MARK: Why are we always so busy telling each other what we'd really like or not like? I'm not really this and you're not really that and we never really one thing and we always really the other. Why don't we go off the really standard for a little while? Really.

JOANNA *picks up the sun-oil squoosher and squirts it over* MARK'*s shoulders in a fancy pattern.*

JOANNA: You're right.

MARK: I'm right?

JOANNA: Baah!

*The* WAITER *comes back with a tray, with two cold lobsters in their red shells.*


## 127. EXT. *DESERTED BEACH. DAY.*

MARK *and* JOANNA *have dozed off. They wake up, beet red. Burned! They look at each other in horror.*


## 128. INT. *HOTEL BEDROOM. DAY.*

MARK *and* JOANNA *stare with horror at their images in the mirror. They are both bright red.*

MARK: What'll we do?

JOANNA: Stand very still. For several days. And maybe it'll go away.

MARK: I don't want to stand very still. I don't want to at all.

*He makes to embrace her.* JOANNA *gives a little scream.*

JOANNA: Nor do I. (*She stares at him.*) Come back next week.

*He leans forward and kisses her gently, their bodies not touching.*

MARK: Did that hurt?

JOANNA *shakes her head. She takes his fingers, one at a time in hers. He leans forward and kisses her again.*

MARK: Scream quietly if I'm hurting.

> *He looks into her eyes. He puts a hand, very gently, to her shoulder. She opens her mouth in a great yell of silent anguish. He takes the hand away. She shakes her head. He puts it back.*

MARK: Joanna, Joanna, Joanna.

JOANNA: That's the first time you've actually said my name as if you meant it.

MARK: Joanna, Joanna, Joanna. I mean it.

> *She smiles ruefully.*

JOANNA: We've only got a week, asbestos.

MARK: I'm not asbestos.

JOANNA: No.

MARK: You're not really going to rejoin those poxy choir-girls, are you?

JOANNA: I promised. We've got a week. A week! (*She speaks as if it were a long time, then – on reflection – as if it were a second.*) Oh … the hell with it. It only hurts for a minute.

*She dives recklessly on to the bed.*


129. EXT. *DALBRETS' VILLA. DAY.*

JOANNA *plunges into the swimming pool.*

*The villa is in good taste, luxurious but not scandalously so.* MAURICE *and* MARK *are playing pingpong very energetically.*

MARK (*smiles across at* JOANNA *as she surfaces*): This is the life, eh darling?

> *She smiles wanly.* MARK *serves and the pingpong resumes.*

MAURICE: Your wife is happy?

MARK: It doesn't take much to make her happy. A villa, a swimming pool, champagne … simple things like that.

> *A couple of* SERVANTS *are lifting a trolley laden with a delicious buffet out on to the terrace.*

MAURICE: You are not angry?

MARK: Angry … ?

MAURICE: Not to be alone together.

MARK: We can always be alone together.

MAURICE: I am waiting now to hear from Palamos about a meeting and then we show you the whole project. If you are interested …

MARK: I'm sure I shall be.

MAURICE: Perhaps it will be necessary to stay a few more days. Shall you mind?

MARK (*grins*): I'll suffer.

> JOANNA *lies back on her towel in the sun by the pool.* MAURICE *slams the ball.*

MAURICE: Game!

> JOANNA *turns at* MAURICE's *cry – hoping it's over – but they change ends with self-absorbed immediacy.*

MARK: Ready?

> *They play.* MAURICE *slams at the ball and it flies high in the air and lands near* JOANNA. *She picks it up.* MARK *turns and claps hands for its return. She holds it up and then takes it to her mouth and makes a great swallowing 'glunk' and holds up empty hands.*

MARK: Come on, darling. Give.

JOANNA: Too late.

> *She points to her stomach.*

MARK (*comes to her – with careful patience*): Sweetheart, we're playing.

JOANNA: Sweetheart, you've been playing for two hours.

> *A* MANSERVANT *has come out carrying a telephone. He plugs the extension cord into the navel of a marble cherub by the pool. The phone immediately rings. The* MANSERVANT *offers it to* MAURICE, *who picks it up.*

MAURICE: Palamos, I was going to call you! Oh! Am I calling you? I understand. Well …

> *He walks off, holding the receiver, followed by the* MANSERVANT *with the bottom part of the phone.*

MARK (*to* JOANNA): Honey, come on, give me the ball.

> MARK *lunges at* JOANNA *and pulls at the towel under which she's hidden the ball.* MARK *grabs.* JOANNA *gets there first. He attacks her. She tosses the ball into the pool, where it floats.*

MARK (*furiously polite*): Will you please get me the ball?

JOANNA: No. It's your game. You get it.

MARK: I have sneakers on. And things.

JOANNA: Very pretty. Françoise lend them to you?

MARK: Yes. They're a guest pair.

JOANNA: Probably her son's.

MARK: Joanna, please get the ball.

JOANNA: Or her grandson's.

MARK: Will you please give up this insane jealousy? I want that ball.

JOANNA: It's there.

> *She points.* MARK *looks furious and glances up at the terrace. Who's watching?*

> MAURICE *is talking on the telephone. He waves to* MARK, *nods into the phone – something is being satisfactorily arranged.*

> *Cut back to* MARK, *who has now grabbed* JOANNA *and picked her up.*

JOANNA: Put me down.

MARK: Will you get me that ball?

JOANNA: Certainly not.

> *He drops her into the pool.*

MARK: Get it.

> JOANNA *gets the ball, dives with it and releases it. It bobs up. Then she swims to the edge of the pool with it and holds it up to* MARK.

> MAURICE *comes down from the terrace.*

MAURICE: We meet Palamos for drinks at six. We talk about the whole scheme and then we make your decision.

MARK: Fine.

*He looks up at* MAURICE *as he reaches for the ball.* JOANNA *grabs his wrist and at the same time braces her legs against the pool side and straightens them.* MARK *is catapulted into the water at great velocity. He comes up spluttering.*

MARK: You little –

JOANNA: You big –

> MARK *and* JOANNA *treading water in the middle of the pool, whispering to each other.*

MARK: Now I've got my shoes wet. I shall probably catch cold.

JOANNA: Mark, how much longer are we going to stay here?

MARK: You got us into this, sugar!

> *He starts up the ladder out of the pool.*

MARK: You were the one who sold me to Maurice. And you were right. A chance like this doesn't come up every day.

JOANNA: Thank God!

> FRANÇOISE *signals to them from the terrace.*

FRANÇOISE: Lunch!

## 130. EXT. *THE TERRACE. DAY.*

MAURICE, *still followed by the* MANSERVANT, *is coming up the steps.*

MAURICE: Six o'clock and I bring the genius with me. Ciao. Ciao.

> *He hangs up. He presses a button and the electric sunshade opens up over the table.*
>
> FRANÇOISE *is gesturing to* MARK *and* JOANNA *to sit down.* FRANÇOISE *presses the bell for the toast, etc. It is next to the awning button.*
>
> JOANNA *sits near the button controls –* FRANÇOISE *tactfully moves round.*

MAURICE: Tonight we all go to the gala and everything is fixed. We see Palamos and …

JOANNA: I don't have any clothes suitable for a gala.

FRANÇOISE: Then I borrow you.
MARK: There you are. Françoise'll borrow you.
FRANÇOISE: I hope you don't mind finishing up the caviare.
MARK: If we must.

> MARK *gives* FRANÇOISE *a boyish grin and then turns to smile at* JOANNA. *She gives him a blindingly false smile in return.*

FRANÇOISE: You like galas?
JOANNA: Some galas.
FRANÇOISE: Would you mind … ?

> *She gestures towards the bell push.*

JOANNA: Not at all.

> *She presses the button – the wrong button. The huge sunshade closes over the entire table and the four of them sitting round it.*

MARK (*from underneath*): Of course that's the trouble with this part of the world. You don't get much of a sunset!

## 131. EXT. *VILLAGE SQUARE. NIGHT.*

*Coloured lights strung up.* COUPLES *are dancing very chastely, à la ball-room. When the music comes to our ears, it is almost unbelievable. Can this be the Hôtel de Paris? No, it cannot! It is eight years earlier. It is the Quatorze Juillet celebrations in the village square. A village band of flatulent amateurishness is playing Dixieland waltzes, while the* PEASANTS *dance their first and last dance of the year. We pick up* JOANNA *and* MARK, *wearing coloured paper hats, as they come on to the 'floor' – actually fenced-off area of the square. We pull back slowly to reveal all this.*

MARK: Joanna, Joanna, Joanna, how can a week go so quickly?
JOANNA: We made the mistake of enjoying it.
MARK: Don't go tomorrow. Just don't.
JOANNA: Let's not go over it again. Let's not.
MARK: All right. We won't.
JOANNA: We agreed.

> *He embraces her – neither dares speak. They dance away from us.*

## 132. INT. *DALBRETS' VILLA. BEDROOM. NIGHT.*

*They shut the door.* JOANNA *is wearing a very chic outfit and a fur wrap which have obviously been borrowed, with her jewellery, from* FRANÇOISE.

JOANNA: Quel gala. Fooof.

*She starts to undress.*

MARK: You were marvellous, Joanna, you were absolutely marvellous.

JOANNA (*looks at herself in the mirror*): I was?

MARK: You were so funny. The way you told the story about the sunshade. You charmed the pants off Palamos.

JOANNA (*slightly drunk*): That would not be too difficult.

*He comes to her and takes her in his arms and looks into her eyes.*

MARK: I knew you'd love it once we got there.

JOANNA: I hated it once we got there.

MARK: Why?

JOANNA: Why? Because I'm tired of being a parasite. Because I want to go. Because I want to be on our own.

*She is in her pyjamas, getting into bed. Still in her diamond tiara.*

MARK: Listen, we haven't been here long.

JOANNA: We've been here month after month for two whole days.

MARK: But I'm going to work for the man.

JOANNA: Well, I'm not. (*She makes a grand, haughty face.*) I'm not. What're we going to call the baby?

MARK: Baby? Um …

JOANNA: Our baby. What're we going to call him?

MARK (*makes a face*): The baby, I guess. Franz Ferdinand?

*He looks at her curiously.*

JOANNA: What is it?

MARK: I'm trying to imagine you fat.

*She suddenly gazes at him.*

MARK: What is it?

JOANNA: I'm trying to imagine you thin.

*JOANNA still has her tiara on.*

MARK: As I always say to the Duchess, if you want to be a duchess, be a duchess. If you want to make love, hats off.

*She puts the tiara on the side table.*


## 133. EXT. *DESERTED BEACH. NIGHT* (*D. for N.*)

*The paper hats from the carnival are flung on the beach, together with their clothes. Naked legs run through and down the beach. Splash. MARK and JOANNA swimming together in the moonlight.*

JOANNA: I'd like to swim all the way to a desert island and never come back.

MARK: I'll never forget tonight as long as I live.

JOANNA: Won't you?

MARK: Tell you what! Ten years tonight, no matter what, I'll meet you here. Right here. Is it a deal?

JOANNA: You'll be building skyscrapers ten miles high by that time. You'll never be able to get down in time.

MARK: I'll always think of this place as us, no matter what. The lonely sea and the sand!


## 134. EXT. *THE SAME. DAY.*

*JOANNA is building an elaborate sand-castle with CAROLINE. For the moment it seems as if the beach is deserted except for them.*

CAROLINE (*looks up*): Here comes Daddy.

*We now cut to include the whole scene. MARK is indeed coming along the beach, but he is accompanied by PALAMOS, an affluent Greek, for ever twiddling a string of worry beads, his slinky blonde mistress, MICHELLE, in a bikini, COMTE and COMTESSE (YVONNE) DE FLORAC, MAURICE, the SITE MANAGER, and a number of SERVANTS carrying canvas chairs, drinks, sunshades etc. The thud and roar of bulldozers and similar noisy machines fill the air. Above the beach we can see a number of large cars parked at the edge of the site. The Triumph Herald is among them.* MARK *waves briefly at* JOANNA *and then begins to demonstrate with lavish gestures the overall plan for the development.* CAROLINE *and* JOANNA *run down to the sea with a bucket to get water for the finishing touches to the castle. As they return they see the bulldozer crash thoughtlessly through the entire careful structure.*

135. EXT. *THE BEACH AND BAY. NIGHT.* (*D. for N.*)
JOANNA *runs over the paper hats, etc. and across the sand and scrambles, who knows where or why, up the rocks. It is ten years earlier again.* MARK *gathers up the paper hats, towels, etc. and follows her.*

MARK: What the hell's the matter with you?

*He runs after her.*

JOANNA: If you think I'm going to wait ten years and then turn up and smile and say what ho –
MARK: Nobody wants you to say what ho –
JOANNA: And say darling –
MARK: Or darling or anything else –
JOANNA: I don't ever want to see you again.

*She breaks free and climbs on up the rocks towards the top of the bay.*

MARK: Then don't.

JOANNA *turns and wails – with comic effect and intention – yet with real anguish.*

JOANNA: I hate you.
MARK: Joanna!

JOANNA *marches determinedly on her way.* MARK *comes crashing after her.*

MARK (*dodging in front of her again*): Listen, we both went into this with our eyes open. Nobody deceived anybody else –

JOANNA *dodges him and flits through the trees.*

MARK: So stop playing the ruined virgin. I've heard the tune before and I didn't like it then. Anyway, you're the one who's

insisting on going back to your damned choir. Joanna ... I don't
want you to go.
JOANNA: Oh yes you do! You want me to turn into a beautiful
memory and the quicker the better.
MARK: Who said anything about beautiful. Will you come here?
JOANNA: I don't ever want to see you again.
MARK: Not much. Ow!
JOANNA: As long as I live.
MARK: Joanna ...
JOANNA: No.
MARK (*calls*): I've decided we should get married. What do you
say?

    *Shock cut:*

JOANNA (*right next to him*): Yes.

    *The frame freezes.*

    *The picture reanimates.*

JOANNA (*sincere*): I won't ever let you down.
MARK: I will you.
JOANNA: I don't care what you do, as long as I've got you.
MARK (*wondering*): Joanna Wallace!
JOANNA: You won't regret it, sir.
MARK: You will.
JOANNA: Never.

## 136. EXT. *BEACH. DAY.*
*The* CHAUFFEUR *opens the boot of the second Rolls Royce and we see
that it contains an ice-bucket with champagne in it. The* CHAUFFEUR
*joins a line of* SERVANTS *who are now setting up a picnic on the beach.
Behind him a* MOTOR-CYCLIST *on a rather rattly motor-cycle drives up.
He is wearing a panama hat and worn shorts, espadrilles and a towelling
shirt. He looks rather shabby and inappropriate.*

FRANÇOISE (*calls from the beach*): David. We're all down here.

## 137. EXT. *THE BEACH. DAY.*
DAVID *approaches.*

FRANÇOISE (*to* CAROLINE): Caroline dear, you and Jean-Louis are going to have lunch with Nanny. Won't that be nice? And then afterwards you can all go to the zoo or something.

> JOANNA *is not very keen about this but* MARK *gives her a look and* CAROLINE, *after a moment's hesitation, goes off with* JEAN-LOUIS *and his starched* NANNY.

FRANÇOISE: David, you are naughty. We were expecting you yesterday.

DAVID: I'm sorry.

FRANÇOISE: Well, you're very naughty. Now who don't you know? You know Nicky and Michelle and the Comte and Comtesse de Florac and Mark. Have you met Joanna? (JOANNA *shakes her head.*) Joanna Wallace, my brother, David.

DAVID: No. (*Shakes hands.*) How are you?

> *He looks at* JOANNA *with a curiously humorous look as if to say that he and she are somehow separate from this band of self-regarding sophisticates.*

MARK: She's bored and overheated and she's got a headache, but otherwise she's fine, thank you very much.

MICHELLE (*flirtatiously*): Mark, you are horrible. I think he's horrible.

PALAMOS: Mark, I have given Michelle an island. You must come when you have finished here and build us a nest.

MICHELLE (*mimicking*): Cuckoo, cuckoo!

PALAMOS: Without a cuckoo.

FLORAC: You'll be lucky, Nikos.

PALAMOS: I am lucky.

> *During this interchange,* DAVID *and* JOANNA *look at each other, obviously sharing a feeling of distaste for this oh-so-funny carry-on. All this time the bulldozer and machines have continued to clack away, though at a slight distance.*

MAURICE: Mark, I must tell you I can't hear myself eat.

> MARK *gestures to the* SITE MANAGER *to kill the noise. As it stops,* JOANNA *and* DAVID *heave a sigh of relief but at the same*

moment MICHELLE *leans over and turns on, as loudly as it will go, a transistor-radio which immediately begins to blare out le hot music from Radio Monte Carlo.*

138. EXT. *SKY AND GROUND (AERIAL SHOT).*
L.S. *GLIDER.*

138a. INT. *GLIDER. DAY.*
JOANNA *sitting next to* DAVID *in a glider. Total silence. He is obviously an expert pilot.* JOANNA *finds the whole thing delicious.*

139. EXT. *SKY. DAY.*
*The glider completes an aerobatic.*

139a. INT. *GLIDER. DAY.*
*They sit there for a moment, then* JOANNA *turns to him and smiles.*
JOANNA: And they never got home to early tea.

140. EXT. *WINDING ROAD. DAY.*
*The Triumph Herald comes careering wildly through the bends. It passes a place with a great broken bridge towering above the road.*

140a. INT. *HERALD. DAY.*
MARK *is driving.*

141. EXT. *RESTAURANT L'ABBAYE. VENCE. DAY.*
*The restaurant is built in the ruins of an old abbey.* MARK *drives the Triumph Herald in and parks it. He walks up the drive.*

142. EXT. *THE RESTAURANT. DAY.*
MARK *comes along.* JOANNA *and* DAVID *are at a table together. From* MARK'S *P.O.V. we hold them in view and the frame freezes for a second to suggest the shock effect on* MARK. *Natural motion resumes as he goes forward to them.*

DAVID *looks up politely.*

DAVID: Good morning. Coffee?

MARK (*looking at* JOANNA): Good morning. Thank you. (*To* JOANNA) Caroline sends her love.

    MARK *draws in a deep breath. The coffee is brought and poured.*

MARK: Did you stay here last night?

DAVID: Yes. It's very comfortable.

MARK: Stayed here before, have you?

DAVID: Once or twice.

    MARK *looks at* JOANNA. *She seems unappalled.* MARK *unwraps sugar and puts it in his coffee.*

MARK (*with final exasperation*): Look, do you think I could have a word with Joanna – alone?

DAVID: But of course!

    *He stands up, moistens his finger and holds it up to the wind. Then he ambles off and leaves them alone.*

## 143. EXT. *THE RESTAURANT. GARDENS. DAY.*
MARK *and* JOANNA *in the old gardens.*

MARK: You slept in the same room.

JOANNA: Yes.

MARK: In other words –

JOANNA: Yes.

MARK: Are you in love?

JOANNA: Yes.

MARK: After only one day – ?

JOANNA: Yes.

MARK: I see.

JOANNA: I'm like that.

MARK: Are you? How many times has this happened, you being like this?

JOANNA: Twice. (*Pause*) You and David.

MARK: I thought I was going to last a lifetime.

    *She shrugs. What can I do?*

JOANNA: I never meant it to happen. We just suddenly found we –

*She shrugs again. How can you explain?*

MARK: Got on?

JOANNA: If you like.

MARK: Oh, I'm absolutely mad about the idea.

*He watches her for a moment.*

DAVID *walks over to* MARK.

DAVID: You really mustn't blame yourself you know.

MARK: You've got your infernal bloody gall, I must say. I don't bloody blame myself. I blame you.

DAVID: But that is ridiculous!

MARK: Look – Joanna's my wife – or had you not heard?

DAVID: This talk of blame is very childish! You have not loved Joanna and now you are angry if someone else does. That is very childish.

MARK: Haven't loved her? I married her.

DAVID: Since some time you have not loved her. I am not taking her away from you, you know.

MARK: Oh?

DAVID: We are simply going away together for a time.

MARK: Thanks. You've set my mind at rest.

DAVID: I'm sorry we did not know each other longer. It would have been easier.

MARK: Oh yes. And more fun! Then you could have had the supreme pleasure of taking your friend's wife. That's real kicks!

## 144. EXT. *THE CAR PARK. L'ABBAYE. DAY.*
MARK *watches* DAVID *get into the Herald with* JOANNA. *The picture goes out of focus. The whole scene is, from* MARK'S *P.O.V. blurred.*

## 144a. EXT. *VILLA TERRACE. DAY.*
MARK *building a house for* CAROLINE *out of bricks. The theme of* MARK *and* CAROLINE *is now, of course, the stronger. He looks at his watch.*

## 145. EXT. *THE SITE. DAY.*

MARK *hurries towards the beach from the Herald and is soon involved directing the unloading of a number of things from a lorry which has driven right down on to the sand.*

MICHELLE *comes into view water-skiing, towed by a motor-boat with one of* PALAMOS's SAILORS *in charge. She is very good at water-skiing, but when she sees* MARK *she waves and allows herself to sink into the water and swims in towards him.*

MICHELLE: Why don't you come out?

> MARK *shakes his head.*

MICHELLE: Palamos won't mind.

> MARK *shakes his head again. She swims back to the skis and fits them on again. She signals to the motor-boat driver who switches on power again. As they go off, she sticks her tongue out at* MARK *who smiles and waves before turning away.*
>
> *A cable has just been fastened to a small gnarled tree and attached to the bulldozer which is obviously going to yank the tree out of the ground.*

MARK: No, not that one. There's still life in it, for God's sake.


## 146. EXT. *ST TROPEZ RESTAURANT. DAY.*

DAVID *and* JOANNA *are finishing lunch at a small restaurant in the old port. The tables are out on the quay.* DAVID *offers* JOANNA *a cigarette, which she accepts and smokes rather self-consciously, to calm her uncertainties.*

DAVID: The whole world is changing out of all recognition – there is no such thing as permanence any more –

> *She turns back to him with a smile. Her thoughts have been elsewhere.*

JOANNA: No, I suppose not.

DAVID: And we should be glad!

JOANNA: Yes, I suppose so.

> *Her eyes go to a middle-aged* COUPLE *sitting morosely staring at the field. She leans forward and indicates them to* DAVID.

DAVID: What sort of people just sit like that without a word to say to each other?

JOANNA (*the old joking answer trips from her tongue*): Married people!

DAVID (*unamused*): Exactly!

JOANNA (*looking at the couple*): It's sad, though.

DAVID: No, my darling, it is not sad. When something is finished, one must say – it's finished. What is sad? What is sad is to go on when there is nothing left. That is sad. Like you and Mark. That is sad.

> *That is sad?* JOANNA *thinks to herself. Then she puts a bold face on it and smiles.*

## 147. EXT. *THE BEACH. NIGHT.*

*After the proposal.* JOANNA *picks up the carnival hats and puts hers on* MARK's *head and his on hers.*

JOANNA: I shall always love you, always, always, no matter what.

MARK (*promise?*): No matter what?

JOANNA (*very naive and sincere*): Yes. (*Pause*) As long as I don't catch you.

> *He embraces her tenderly. He pulls the hat right down over her face. She puts out her arms like blind man's buff.*

MARK: If you can catch me, you can keep me.

## 148. EXT. *FORK IN ROAD. DAY.*

DAVID *and* JOANNA *are sitting inside the parked Herald.*

DAVID: There comes a time when one must grow. When the old things are not amusing any more.

> JOANNA *does not answer.*

## 149. EXT. *A BEACH. DAY.*

MARK *and* JOANNA *playing beach cricket.* MARK *bowls – with a rubber ball – and hits* JOANNA, *batting with a piece of driftwood, on the leg. A hunk of dried cactus as wicket.*

MARK: How was that?

JOANNA: Painful.

MARK: That was out, you pregnant sow. That was plumb out. Leg before cactus.

JOANNA (*advances on him*): Pregnant what?

>*He runs into the sea.*

JOANNA (*sits down*): You'll have to come out eventually and then I'll –

>*She settles determinedly and looks round.*

MARK: Help!

>*She looks up. He is going under the water.*

MARK: If you don't forgive me, I'll drown myself.

>*He goes dramatically under again.*

JOANNA (*alarmed*): Mark. Come back, all is forgiven.

>MARK *gives a fearful gurgling scream and goes down again, spouting water.*

MARK: Too late!

JOANNA (*screams*): Mark –

>*She plunges into the water. He stands up. In water up to his shins.*

MARK (*the butler*): You called?

JOANNA: Bastard!

>*He makes a funny face and jerks towards her, walking like some bizarre thing from outer space. He looms up over* JOANNA.

MARK (*in a monstrous voice*): Give us a kiss.


150. EXT. *FORK IN ROAD. DAY.*

JOANNA *smiles to herself, almost laughing. Then she looks across.* DAVID *is not smiling. She takes the smile off her face.*

DAVID: Well?

>*He turns to her, sympathetic but somehow distant.*

DAVID: You must decide.

JOANNA: I know.

>*He puts his arm round her and draws her to him.*

DAVID: If something is dead, the best thing is to bury it. The quicker the better.
JOANNA: Yes.


## 151. INT. *BEDROOM. DALBRET VILLA. EVENING.*

MARK *lying on the bed, surrounded with drawings on which he affects to be working. He looks at his watch. He leans over the papers. He looks up at the door.*

*A movement. He looks at the terrace door. And there is* JOANNA.


## 151a. EXT. *FORK IN ROAD. DAY.*

JOANNA *kissing* DAVID.


## 152. INT. *BEDROOM. DALBRET VILLA. EVENING.*

JOANNA, *dressed as in the last scene, comes towards* MARK.

MARK: Hullo.
JOANNA: Hullo.
MARK: Well?
JOANNA: I'm back.
MARK: Enjoy yourselves?
JOANNA (*nods, looking hard at him*): Yes, thank you. But I missed you.
MARK: (*mirthless laugh*): Ha!
JOANNA: I did.
MARK: Why?
JOANNA (*shrugs*): He was so serious.
MARK: I thought you liked people to be serious.
JOANNA: But he was so serious.
MARK: Remind me to make some funny faces.
JOANNA: You don't need to make them.
MARK: Ha!
JOANNA: Mark, I'm back.
MARK: You humiliate me. You humiliate me and then – you come back.
JOANNA: That's right.

MARK: Thank God!

> *He grabs her and embraces her. She looks into his face, searching for something and then accepts his kiss, almost frightened, not knowing whether it will work or whether she should yield again to him so quickly.*

> *She kisses him fervently, eyes shut.*

MARK: You're sure you remember which one I am?

> *She looks sick. She twists out of his arms and runs, panting and sobbing, out of the terrace window.* MARK *is appalled at what he has said and frightened that he has lost her again by his silly gibe.*

153. EXT. *THE GARDEN OF THE VILLA. EVENING.*
*The sun is setting, golden light fills the gardens.* JOANNA *runs down the steps of the terrace and in among the bushes and flowers.*

MARK: Joanna –

> *He blunders on through the bushes.* JOANNA *moves away.*

MARK: Joanna –

> MARK's P.O.V. *He sees her behind a barrier of low bushes. He flings himself through the bushes towards her.*

> *The swimming pool is between him and her. He goes hurtling into the pool at great speed and with an enormous splash.*

> JOANNA *breaks up.*

> MARK *breaks surface and looks at her with a bleak, drowning expression.*

> *She comes down to the edge of the pool and holds out her hand to him. He climbs out of the pool and stands there.*

JOANNA: You'd better come inside. You're raining.
MARK: I've been a fool. A great big fool.
JOANNA: We've both …
MARK: It's all been me really. You were always … (*He stops and shrugs*) I'm sorry.
JOANNA: Forget it.
MARK: Can we forget it?

JOANNA: Can you?

MARK: I can. I'm just glad you're back. That's all I care about.

JOANNA: Well, I'm back.

MARK: Well that's all I care about.

*They go in.*

## 153a. EXT. *AUTOROUTE. MERCEDES. DAY.*

*The last frames of the last scene are visible in the driving mirror of the Mercedes as* MARK *and* JOANNA *pull away from the Plage and speed away up the autoroute. The images fall away as if they were the images of something they have overtaken. Both of them glance at the mirror and then at each other, balefully.*

MARK: We should've parted then.

JOANNA: Why didn't we?

MARK: I didn't have the courage.

JOANNA: You didn't have the courage? What courage did you need?

MARK: The courage to see that what was finished was finished.

JOANNA: And what was finished?

MARK: You know bloody well what was finished.

JOANNA: Yes, I do. Me and David. And we finished. So?

MARK: I should have left you to it. It would have hurt – but that's what I should have done. Only I didn't have the courage. It would have meant going back to a life of joyless promiscuity; an endless succession of purely physical relationships, traipsing from one bed to another, brief affairs with a row of brainless birds with nothing but their bodies to offer. No wonder my nerve failed me. It would've needed a man of iron to face that prospect without wavering. Right?

*He smiles at her, his good humour somewhat restored, as usual, by a bold flight of the imagination.*

JOANNA: What the hell do you want?

MARK: My cake and eat it. Doesn't everybody?

*A pause.*

MARK: You know as well as I do you're hoping he'll be there. Why pretend?

JOANNA: I'm not pretending. I do hope he'll be there.

MARK: You see?

JOANNA: I like him. And it'll give me someone to talk to when Maurice drags you off for one of his ten-minute chats for six hours.

MARK: I'm not having any ten-minute chats with Maurice.

JOANNA: Ha!

MARK (*mock Continental*): I swear to you.

*We see a sign: 'CAP VALÉRY – NEXT EXIT'.*

MARK: Pin on a nice smile. We're almost there.

*JOANNA pins on a nice smile, radiantly false.*

## 154. INT. *DE FLORAC VILLA. NIGHT.*

MARK *and* JOANNA, *now looking radiant, come up to* YVONNE *and* HUSBAND *carrying the statue.*

MARK: Joanna thought he'd make a handsome addition to the living-pit.

YVONNE: Bless you both. (*She kisses* JOANNA) Prettier than ever! (*and then she kisses* MARK.)

MARK: Prettier than ever?

YVONNE (*with a light laugh*): Everyone is admiring the house so much – I can't tell you.

MARK: Tell me, tell me. I can't stand praise unless I have it.

AMERICAN LADY: You must be the architect. I just love the high ceilings.

MARK: And the low floors?

AMERICAN LADY: Precious!

*As* MARK *is being congratulated and generally lionized, he (and we) see* DAVID *come in from the terrace. He sees* JOANNA *and gives her a slow smile. She smiles at him and there is a sudden swoop of feeling between them, of which* MARK, *surrounded by flattery, is only too conscious.*

*There are many guests in the house and music is playing.* JOANNA *and* DAVID *approach each other and, without our hearing any-*

*thing, embrace, kiss on either cheek, smiling, unnoticed by anyone apparently, except* MARK *who notices all right.*

DAVID *takes* JOANNA *by the arm and leads her out of the terrace door.*

AMERICAN LADY (*over this*): You'll never believe this – it's just the wildest coincidence imaginable – but right when I was en route [*on root*] to the airport who should I bump into – metaphorically, of course –

MARK (*watching* DAVID *and* JOANNA): Of course.

AMERICAN LADY: ... but Howard and Cathy Maxwell Manchester on the way home from the hospital where she's been undergoing surgery for a particularly nasty cyst although I'm glad to say the doctors have given her a very hopeful prognosis and they said I should call you up when I got to Europe and what a darling couple you were and then when I called Yvonne and discovered that you'd built their new home for them, well, you can imagine –

MARK: Yes.

AMERICAN LADY: Isn't it just the wildest coincidence imaginable?

MARK: What? Oh yes, yes, isn't it?

AMERICAN LADY: I think you've done the most fantastic things. I guess you must be a very happy man.

MARK: I guess so.

AMERICAN LADY (*laughs*): That's right. And your wife's so darling. I've heard a lot about her. And you've got a wonderful little boy, haven't you?

MARK (*blinks*): We've got a wonderful little girl, actually.

MARK *moves to get away.*

AMERICAN LADY: Enjoy it while you have it – that's my advice. My husband recently passed on, you know, and believe me, you don't know what you've had until you don't have it any more. Still and all, it makes me very happy to see a really talented young man break right through to the top and I only wish Howard and Cathy were here right now to see it because, believe me, I know, they always believed in you right from the first, if not before …

*Through the terrace window, without being able to hear them, we and* MARK *have seen glimpses of* DAVID *and* JOANNA, *smiling and talking together.* MARK *now manages to slip away from the* AMERICAN LADY *and moves across towards the buffet which lies between him and the terrace door. The* AMERICAN LADY'S *voice goes right on talking, as above, although* MARK *has now slipped the leash of her garrulity.*

*Now* MARK *sees* JOANNA *look suddenly delighted. She spreads her arms and kisses* DAVID *enthusiastically.* MARK *feels sick. He puts down the plate of food which a* WAITER *has handed him and pours himself a glass of wine which he drains instantly.*

*He puts the glass down and starts for the terrace. A* SERVANT *touches his arm. He turns and sees that the* MAN *is carrying a telephone.*

SERVANT: Monsieur Wallace?

MARK *nods.*

SERVANT: Telephone for you.

MARK (*takes it*): Thank you very much.

SERVANT: One moment – I plug you in.

MARK (*to a very* PRETTY GIRL *whom we shall know as* SYLVIA): One moment, he plugs me in.

MARK *follows, still carrying the phone, to a corner where there is a plug.*

SERVANT: They call you from America.

MARK: They call me from America. They call me from here. They call me from there. They call me from every bloody where.

SYLVIA *smiles with slow amusement.*

MARK (*into phone*): Hullo? Hal! Hallo, how are you? (*Excited, to* SYLVIA, *forgetting she isn't* JOANNA) It's Hal Van Benius. (*Into phone*) Well, what's the story? You do! It's fixed? Well, that's wonderful.

134

*All this time he is trying to see out of the terrace door. He stretches the cord to its limit.*

MARK: When do we start? (*laughs*) Yesterday I can't do. I already have things I have to do yesterday.

*He makes a 'big deal' face at* SYLVIA, *who again smiles.*

MARK: Rome! You are? When? Friday? I'll be there. I'll be there. I've got it. See you then. Great.

*He puts the phone down.*

MARK: Rome on Friday.

SYLVIA: So, you are very much the success.

MARK: Incredibly much. Shall we dance?

*She nods slowly. There are a couple of other couples dancing. Nothing elaborate.* MARK *dances* SYLVIA *towards the terrace. The lights flicker for a moment and there is a gasp of excitement and then they steady again.*

SYLVIA: I think it is too early in the evening for that.

MARK: Is it ever too early in the evening for that?

*He smiles roguishly and she seems to enjoy it. He feels better.*

MAURICE *is now seen coming into the room, wiping his hands.*

MAURICE: Mark – you are here! No one tells me a thing. I am repairing the electrics, which you should have been here to check again incidentally, and no one tells me you are arriving.

MAURICE *has paid not the smallest attention to* SYLVIA *but has come straight between her and* MARK, *whom he takes by the arm.*

MAURICE: I have a great many things now we must discuss.

MARK: You haven't met my fiancée.

MAURICE: How do you do? Now, we go somewhere quiet and have a long talk.

MARK: I thought I'd come to a party.

MAURICE: Please, I have problems. What is your fiancée's name?

MARK: I don't know. I'll ask her. Excuse me, darling, what's your name?

SYLVIA (*enjoying the charade*): Sylvia.

135

MAURICE: She's very pretty. (*Frowns*) You have divorced Joanna? (*He is suddenly aware of what's been said.*) I don't understand! Anyway, the main question is, when are you free?

> DAVID *and* JOANNA *come in through the terrace door.* SYLVIA *still has her arm on* MARK's *shoulder and he has an arm round her waist.* MARK *and* JOANNA *look at each other.* JOANNA *and* DAVID *come towards them;* MAURICE *looks uneasy and uncertain.*
>
> SYLVIA *leaves go of* MARK *and goes and kisses* DAVID *with some passion, which he returns.* MARK *looks astonished,* MAURICE *even more so.*

DAVID (*introducing* SYLVIA *to* JOANNA): Joanna, I want you to meet my fiancée, Sylvia Urbino – Joanna Wallace.

JOANNA: David's been telling me about you.

> MAURICE *is even more astonished.*

MARK: Congratulations.

> *He holds out his hand to* DAVID.

DAVID: Thank you.

MARK (*to* JOANNA): Hal Van Benius just phoned.

JOANNA: And?

MARK (*American accent*): I got the job.

JOANNA: Good! (*isn't it?*) Good?

> *She looks really delighted. He shrugs – yes, it's good.*

MAURICE: You are going to the States?

MARK: Only for a couple of years.

MAURICE: Then you give me ten minutes now. I need your advice.

MARK (*to* JOANNA): We're meeting him in Rome on Friday on his way through.

MAURICE: Ten minutes.

> JOANNA *and* MARK *look at each other.* MAURICE *is up to his old tricks.*
>
> *The* AMERICAN LADY *now comes up with* FRANÇOISE, *beaming.*

AMERICAN LADY (*to* DAVID): Your sister has just been telling me your wonderful news. About you and this beautiful girl.

DAVID *smiles uneasily.*

AMERICAN LADY: Well, all I want to say is, if you can be as happy as these two wonderful young people and have a marriage like theirs, you don't have a thing to worry about.

MARK *and* DAVID *look at each other and a reluctant flicker of amusement passes between them.*

DAVID: I hope very much you are right.

MAURICE: Now, Mark, my problem is very simple but very complicated ... So if you can spare me just ten minutes ...

JOANNA *shakes her head.* MARK *shrugs. What can he do?*

MAURICE: You are the obvious man, since it was your original conception –

*The lights go out very suddenly and very completely. Cries of surprise and alarm.*

MAURICE: Everybody jump please.

*Everybody jumps. The lights come on.*

MAURICE: I think it only fair that you should see what you can do. I am sorry that you are not here to supervise the whole thing, but ten minutes surely is not very much ...

*He looks.* MARK *has gone.* JOANNA *has gone.* DAVID *and* SYLVIA *are smiling at each other. The* AMERICAN LADY *looks puzzled at* MAURICE. MAURICE *and she shrug and, almost without realizing what they are doing, dance off together.*

## 155. EXT. *PINEWOODS. NIGHT.*

*The Mercedes coming slowly down the drive which now leads through the wood to the new villa. We can hear the music from the party.*

MARK: I hate these occasions.

JOANNA: I hate these occasions. You love these occasions.

MARK: I love you.

JOANNA: I love you.

MARK: Hmmm.

JOANNA: How long is this going to go on?

MARK: I don't know. How long is this going to go on?

JOANNA (*brightly*): For ever! (*appalled*) For ever? How long is what going to go on?

MARK *stops the car.*

MARK: You used to think I wasn't ever serious. Now you're never serious.

JOANNA (*seriously*): How long is what going to go on?

MARK: The pretence that we're happy.

JOANNA: You've never pretended we were happy! So who's pretending?

MARK: You are. That you want to stay with me. That we're happily married.

JOANNA: Those are two entirely different things!

MARK: You don't have to tell me.

JOANNA: You really want it all to be a failure, don't you?

MARK: I haven't got anyone else to go to.

JOANNA: You've got women all over the place who'd be glad to renew their subscriptions.

MARK: But I wouldn't be glad.

*He restarts the car.*

JOANNA: If you had someone you wanted to go to, you'd be on your way, you don't have to tell me.

MARK: Then why are you still here?

JOANNA: Because I'm not you.

MARK: How long are you going to go on resenting the past?

JOANNA: Who's talking? Just who is talking?

*He stops the car.*

MARK: I'm talking. What would you do if we got a divorce?

JOANNA: Cry.

MARK: Like for how long?

JOANNA: You want dates? I don't know. Why should we get a divorce?

MARK: Or if I died. If I didn't exist.

JOANNA: Look, if I hadn't had chickenpox, I'd've had chickenpox. I don't know.

MARK (*touches her forehead*): You scratched.

JOANNA: I scratched.

MARK: I love you, Joanna Wallace.

JOANNA: Well then! Well then!

> *He restarts the car.*

MARK: What would you do if I didn't exist?

JOANNA: The trouble with your examination is I have to answer every question.

MARK: It's a tough school.

JOANNA: I'd probably have married David.

> MARK *looks at her with bleak anguish and stops the car.*

JOANNA: But you do exist. You knew the answer, why did you ask the question?

MARK: Because I knew the answer.

JOANNA: There'll never be anyone else like you in my life.

MARK: You promise?

JOANNA: I hope.

MARK (*starts the car*): I thought we were going to be serious.

JOANNA: Serious isn't solemn. I am serious.

> *The car starts to move forward down through the woods.*

JOANNA: It's you who can't accept it.

> MARK *stops the car again.*

JOANNA: Why do you always stop the car as soon as I say anything?

MARK: What can't I accept?

JOANNA: That we're a fixture. That we're married. You go on about me leaving you when I'm always still here. Are you sure you don't want me to leave you?

MARK: Positive.

JOANNA: Michelle's at the party, you know.

MARK: Positive.

JOANNA: Suddenly you're a vegetarian?

MARK: You are my meat.

JOANNA: And so are you mine. (MARK *starts the car again.*) Why do you think I'm here?

MARK: I don't know. That's the whole –

JOANNA: That's the whole thing, you never stop to think.

*MARK stops the car again.*

MARK: I've stopped. To think.

JOANNA: Stop thinking.

*She puts her arms round him and kisses him. She whispers to him. He looks at her.*

MARK: Now?

*She nods.*

MARK: Here?

*She nods again, vigorously.*

JOANNA: I love happy endings!

*He smiles at her and kisses her passionately, all in one.*

MARK: You're just plain immoral.

JOANNA: How can it be immoral if you're married?

MARK: We're going to have to get a divorce.

## 156. EXT. *THE COAST ROAD. DAY.*

JOANNA *and* MARK *in their hitch-hiking days are walking steadily along the road.*

*They turn and look back and see a car coming.* MARK *raises his thumb.*

*The Ford with the* MAXWELL MANCHESTERS *in it slows down and they get in.*

*The Ford goes away from us and suddenly pulls in and stops.*

*Speeded-up action: The* OCCUPANTS *of the Ford change places and the car moves off again.*

## 157. EXT. *TRAFFIC LIGHTS. SAME DAY.*

*The Ford slows down. The M.G. pulls in next to it, on the far side (we*

*cannot see into the driving seat). The lights change, the Ford pulls away
quickly. The M.G. moves more slowly. We see now that in fact* MARK
*and* JOANNA *are pushing it from behind.*

*There is a loud hoot. They look up indignantly. The Herald with them
aboard, comes up with them. They stop pushing the M.G., which rolls
backwards out of shot, and climb into their own selves in the Herald.*

## 158. EXT. *ROUNDABOUT. SAME DAY.*
*The Herald comes along with two of them sitting in front, rather coldly.
At the roundabout, cut to:*

*Top shot: The Herald splits into two identical Heralds, one of which goes
one way, following a Saab with a blonde in it, the other the other way with*
JOANNA *and* DAVID *in it.*

*The two cars meet at the far side of the roundabout and rejoin into one.*
JOANNA *and* MARK *are reunited.*

*The Mercedes immediately overtakes the Herald. We stay with the
Mercedes and see* MARK *and* JOANNA *driving along 'in the present'
smiling and in good humour.*

## 159. EXT. *THE FRENCH-ITALIAN FRONTIER. DAY.*
*The Mercedes snaking up the steep approach to the frontier station.*

MARK (*philosophizing*): We've changed. You have to admit it.
JOANNA: I admit it. We've changed.
MARK: It's sad, but there it is. Life.
JOANNA: It's not that sad. Do you know what I dreamt? I
dreamt –
MARK: This is no time for triplets. (*He smiles.*) Maybe there are
compensations. Monster!
JOANNA: Well at least you're not a bad-tempered, disorganized,
conceited failure any more.

> *They have reached the barrier area.*

MARK: No, I'm a pretty slick fellow in my way.

> *He flips open the glove compartment and hands out documents to the*
> OFFICIALS.

JOANNA: You're a bad-tempered, disorganized, conceited success.

MARK: Thank you. And you are no longer a suburban nobody. You're a suburban somebody! Who says I'm disorganized?

*He files the returned documents neatly.*

OFFICIAL: Passeport.

MARK, *smiling still, flips open another compartment and reaches in, but there is nothing. He looks unruffled. He pats his pocket confidently, but again there is nothing. He starts to get out of the car – but his seat belt is fastened. He unhooks it, slightly flustered now, and gets out. He pats himself furiously, looks under the car, under the seat – rushes round and opens the boot.*

*We lift and pull back from the scene.* MARK *is increasingly flapped. He starts to rave.*

MARK: I've got to get to Rome. I've got a very important meeting – I have to get through – I don't know what's happened to it, but –

OFFICIALS *are gesticulating and shrugging.*

*As this drama reaches its peak,* JOANNA *is once more holding up the missing passport. She looks at* MARK. *He stops in mid-rhetoric and looks at her ruefully. He takes the passport and hands it to the* OFFICIAL.

MARK: Passeport.

*He comes up to* JOANNA *and takes her in his arms and kisses her once more.*

MARK: Bitch.
JOANNA: Bastard.

*Fade out.*

## THE END